WALKING TOUR OF WALDEN TWO

WALKING TOUR OF WALDEN TWO

A Student's Guidebook

L. Dodge Fernald
Harvard University

Illustrations by Brian W. Dow

Macmillan Publishing Company
NEW YORK

Macmillan Publishing Company
866 Third Avenue, New York, New York 10022

Collier Macmillan Canada, Inc.

Printing: 1 2 3 4 5 6 7   Year: 9 0 1 2 3 4 5

ISBN 0-02-337030-0

"I preferred to spend the time instead in a little walking tour, every step of which would bring me closer to Walden Two."

—*Burris*

Contents

Foreword

In a recent study of the utopias and anti-utopias written during the past century,[1] *Walden Two* was singled out as a "methodological utopia." It not only portrayed a way of life that was free of many of the things we object to in the world today, it claimed to show how such a life could be arranged. I wrote the book in 1945 just as the Second World War was coming to an end. We had not yet learned the worst about the Nazi regime and the atom bomb had not yet been dropped on Hiroshima, but it was clear that it was time to think about a better world.

Eight years earlier I had published another book [2] in which I reported some laboratory research (if only with white rats) where, under certain conditions, behavior was fairly precisely controlled. In that book I refused to consider what control could mean outside the laboratory ("Let him extrapolate who will," I said), but the war had made it clear that extrapolation might be worthwhile. Something might be done to build a better way of life.

Some of the things I thought could be done were these: Children could be raised and educated much more successfully and better prepared for the world in which they would live as adults. Unpleasant work could be reduced to a minimum, and work conditions could be made more enjoyable. Personal relations could be improved by reducing the need for possessive and competitive behavior. There would be much more room for the enjoyable things of life.

I have been surprised by how many other advantages now seem to follow from the way of life portrayed in *Walden Two*. The community is minimally consuming. There is very little waste. The resources of the earth are modestly consumed. It is a way of life that is minimally polluting. Although women have babies at an earlier age (I would change that today) there are many fewer reasons to have children (for example, as helpers, as additional sources of income, as support in old age, and so on) and greater opportunities to enjoy children whether or not they are one's own. A world of Walden Twos would be much less likely to need nuclear weapons.

Of course, the design of any way of life raises problems. For one thing, it suggests an authoritarian figure who controls everyone's behavior. I discuss issues of that kind in *Walden Two* as I discussed them with a group of friends during the war. (One character in the book is close to one of those friends.)

Whatever the danger in design, the greater danger is in doing nothing. Walden Two is a sample of one kind of thing that might be done, and it will be no great loss if its principal effect is to suggest other ways.

B. F. Skinner

---

1 Krishan Kumar, *Utopia and Anti-Utopia in Modern Times*. Oxford: Basil Blackwood, Ltd., 1987

2 B. F. Skinner, *The Behavior of Organisms*. New York, Appleton Century, 1938.

Preface

This guidebook celebrates the fortieth anniversary of the publication of *Walden Two*. It offers a series of illustrations, definitions, summaries, and exercises describing B. F. Skinner's utopian community.

It can be used before or after reading *Walden Two*. Or it can be read on a unit-by-unit basis, simultaneously with the comparable sections of that book. All numbers in parentheses in this guidebook refer to pages in the 1976 reissued edition of *Walden Two*, except for those at the ends of the summaries, which refer to chapters.

These materials might have been prepared by T. E. Frazier or any other member of Walden Two, eager to describe the community to other interested persons. But instead it was the author's privilege and pleasure to earn his labor credits in this way.

LDF
Cambridge, MA

Part One
The Tours

"'It has become a tradition among our sheep never to approach string. The lambs acquire it from their elders, whose judgment they never question.'"

Unit I
Breaking Away
(Chapters 1-3)

This unit introduces six characters in search of a utopia and foreshadows their different viewpoints. It also gives a brief glimpse of the Walden Two community.

Summary

After their discharge from military service, Lieutenant Rogers invites his friend, Steve Jamnik, to visit his college campus. They meet Professor Burris, his former psychology instructor, and Rogers explains that they are in search of a place for themselves in contemporary society. But they do not want to begin again in their earlier ways. After fighting a war, they want to start fresh in life, to experiment, to try new ways of living.

"Why not get some people together and set up a social system somewhere that will really work?" Rogers asks his former professor. "There are a lot of things about the way we're all living now that are completely insane—"

In particular, the young men want to locate the author of a magazine article on an experimental community apparently much like one that Professor Burris discussed in his psychology classes years earlier. It turns out that Burris, some time ago, did know this author, T. E. Frazier. He agrees to write to Frazier, asking if this experimental community, Walden Two, is still in existence and if it still accepts visitors. (Chapter 1)

❦❧❦❧❦❧

The potential touring party becomes larger when two young women join. Barbara Macklin is Rogers' fiancee, and Mary Grove is a friend of Steve Jamnik. Moreover, Professor Burris has met a colleague from the Philosophy Department, skeptical Augustine Castle. Fascinated by thoughts of ideal societies, Castle immediately accepts an invitation to visit, making a group of six altogether.

In the meantime, Rogers has found Frazier's article. It emphasizes that political activity is of little use in building a better world. Instead, economic self-sufficiency can be obtained with modern technology, and the psychological problems of group living can be managed through the principles of "behavioral engineering."

The group leaves on Wednesday, planning to spend the rest of the week on this adventure. After a trip by train and bus, they are met by Frazier at a deserted bus stop. He is simply dressed and wears a scarcely visible beard.

The ride in his station wagon takes them from the main highway through prosperous farm lands, by typical farmhouses and barns, and then to a series of buildings of a different sort, earth-colored, built of rammed earth and stone. Arranged in levels and connected in wings and extensions, these buildings, part of Walden Two, follow the landscape in a functional design.

Taken to their rooms in pairs—the young women, young men, and two professors—they find them small and functional, with large windows, all much alike. Printed bedspreads, wood with natural finish, and earth-colored walls set the tone. After surveying their room, Burris and Castle take an unexpected nap. (Chapter 2)

"We shall have fifty or sixty hours together," says Frazier upon awakening them. "What do you say to a leisurely start?"

Their walk takes them first by an expanse of cropped grass. Frazier explains that the sheep cut the grass. The flock is kept together, as a movable lawnmower, by a length of string stretched to form an enclosure. The training of the sheep to stay together in one area began with a portable electric fence, but soon it was clear that the fence need not be electrified. The sheep kept well away from it anyway, and so a piece of string is used instead, much easier to move when a new patch of grass needs cutting.

The new lambs, Frazier explained, never question the judgment of their elders. They adopt the same habit.

Burris and Castle object that some day a skeptical lamb will put his nose to the string, receive no shock, and begin a stampede. The whole sheep society will be disrupted. But the tradition, Frazier explains, is also due to the Bishop, a quiet sheepdog near the flock.

They pass a clear pond, reclaimed from a swamp by the medical staff and now suitable for swimming. They enter a pine grove which screens the workshops from living quarters. Then they observe some birches which separate the gardens and pastures. Frazier takes pleasure in pointing out these small but successful "treaties with nature."

Then all the interconnected main buildings come into view, built at low cost with rammed earth and stone, accommodating the one thousand members of Walden Two. The construction offers cooperative housing and ready access from all personal rooms to the dining room, theater, and living rooms. If the Walden Two community were constructed in contemporary buildings, Frazier explains, it would occupy perhaps two hundred and fifty houses and one hundred offices and warehouses. The savings in time and money are significant.

In addition, the connections among these buildings offer protection against the weather. The streets of Edward Bellamy's Boston of the future, Frazier reminds his listeners, would be covered when it rained.

Most significant among these buildings is the Ladder, a long passageway connecting the children's quarters and the main room. It was once called Jacob's Ladder, for it allows the little angels to go up and down the stairs. With large windows, it has several stages and alcoves furnished with chairs and tables. The children and adults traveling from one place to another can stop here and enjoy themselves in small groups for snacks, rest, readings, conversation, or the magnificent view.

Frazier speaks proudly of the Walden Two architects. He explains that their contributions to the community could hardly be exaggerated. (Chapter 3)

Key Concepts

Write a definition for each of these terms. When in doubt, reread the indicated pages in *Walden Two* and consult the glossary in this guidebook.

utopian community, 2

experiment, 5

behavioral engineering, 10

cooperative housing, 19

control of weather, 19

the "Ladder," 20

Illustrations

The concepts in *Walden Two* are often illustrated in daily life. Below are students' illustrations of three concepts in this unit. Supply additional examples yourself of these or other key concepts in this unit.

Experiment (5). "After successfully completing a six-month drug rehabilitation program I returned to my parents' home. Feeling frightened and self-conscious among old and potential new friends, I secluded myself and kept my interaction with others to a minimum.

"I became frustrated and unhappy with this unnatural feeling of introversion, so I decided to experiment with ways to draw myself out.

"I tried using the phone a bit and felt somewhat better. Then I used it more often. Writing letters also made me feel more a part of things. There was a housecat that everybody ignored. I made friends with it but that didn't seem to help. I needed human contact.

"I selected and wore clothes that were attractive. They gave me a boost.

"As a most important step to get a better hold on my self-confidence, I tried using a latent massage talent. I took classes, became certified, and started a successful business.

"I think it's right to stress the importance of experimenting with one's own life and mixing or sharing with others."

Behavioral engineering (10). "My family spent the summer of my second year in a house on the beach. All of my half-sisters, who did not live with me during the year, came too. The excitement of a broken routine and the added attention I was receiving had somewhat disturbed my sleep patterns. After much protest I would reluctantly go to bed but I would be unable to fall asleep. I cried until someone came to pick me up, and then I spent the evening happily basking in the attention of my family.

"Rapidly tiring of this routine, my parents devised an evil plan. One night they instructed my sisters to let me cry—to teach me to go to sleep without a fuss. The family gathered in the living room to guard each other from any unwise sympathy that might sabotage the scheme. I called out to all of them: 'Help me! Save me Martie! Save me Susie! Save me Glenda! Mommy, Daddy help me!' I cried and I screamed and I appealed to their softer side, but in the interest of family peace they ignored my pleas. Eventually, I drifted off to sleep forsaking the possibility of rescue.

"The next night my parents told me that I could stay up fifteen minutes later because I had not gotten out of bed the night before—and I enjoyed that privilege. In fact, my parents let me stay up fifteen minutes more every night because ever afterward I went to sleep without complaining. They claim that I never again called out to be saved from the cruel fate of sleep."

Control of weather (19). "I was once a privileged guest at a monastery in the wilds of New York State. For two weeks, I found myself in a remote, completely self-contained unit, perhaps the only one of this sort in North America. There was no interference from the outside world, even from the weather.

"The six major buildings were designed to interact with one another. They faced towards the center of a small open area, two buildings on each side, one at each end. Made of stone from a nearby quarry, and built in a low, secluded valley, they will be there for a *long* time.

"The most interesting part of this construction, for me, was the way the buildings allowed life to continue completely uninterrupted by the heat, cold, rain, or snow. All of them were connected by enclosed corridors, with alcoves in the hallways. Each dormitory room opened onto one of these hallways, passing right through the center of each building. Both the rooms and halls contained large picture windows, giving an awesome view of the mountains, letting in a large amount of light and, when the sun shone, heat as well.

"With no significant interference from any 'outside forces,' including the elements, contemplation and prayer continued in smooth fashion, never off schedule. This design of the buildings gave some control over the weather; it allowed monastic life to go on without any such concerns."

Study Questions

1. Note the first impressions of Frazier—his manner, dress, greeting, and the station wagon. What do they suggest about Walden Two? What care should be taken in forming such hypotheses? (11)

2. After turning off the main highway and passing some traditional farmhouses and barns, the visitors notice a series of buildings, Walden Two. Briefly, describe them. What is the general structure or plan of these buildings? (12)

3. The sheep follow their elders, staying away from the harmless string. The Bishop, the watchdog, is also there to keep them from straying. Draw an analogy to human civilization, using both parts of this illustration, the harmless string and the dog. (15)

4. Frazier says, "The pond is our own work." What does he mean? What evidence supports this practice today? (17)

5. How many people live in the Walden Two community? Why is it advantageous to work with a group of this size in establishing a utopian society? In your answer, refer to the concept of experimentation. (18)

6. Describe the architecture and housing in Walden Two. How do they reflect modern trends in home construction? What are the reasons behind the Walden Two approach? (18)

7. What is done about adverse weather in Walden Two? To what extent is this method used today in large cities? With what result? (19)

8. How is the Ladder involved in the control of weather? The social development of children? Recreation? (20)

9. What is the attitude toward seniority at Walden Two? Why? Note that the full answer to this question is revealed in later discussions of history and personal figures. (21)

10. Frazier says, "But imagine what it would mean to an architect to design an entire community as a whole!" Explain Frazier's view, focusing not only upon the size but also on the demands of the job, as opposed to designing a small part of the more traditional environment. (22)

Values Clarification

As the tour begins, Frazier becomes more vocal. He gives a frank opinion on several topics:

1. On the lawnmower: "The stupidest machine ever invented—for one of the stupidest purposes." (15)

2. On the natural environment: "The pond is our own work. It covers some swamp land and stores a bit of water against a dry spell." (17)

3. On cooperative housing: "It's an enormous simplification and a great saving of time and money." (19)

4. On the weather: "It's only when we conquer the weather, or move to a favorable climate, that we understand its tyranny." (19)

Think carefully about these topics. Think about Frazier's remarks. Make some notes on your own reactions.

Circle the number of the topic most important to *you*, regardless of Frazier's comment. Place an "X" over the number of the topic you consider least important, again ignoring Frazier's remark. Then develop an argument supporting the topic you identified as most important, or supporting one of the topics not crossed out, indicating your opinion, the reasons for it, and a refutation of counterarguments.

When we think carefully about topics important to us, perhaps deciding among several possibilities, the process is called values clarification. The aim of values clarification is to help people become aware of their attitudes, beliefs, and feelings about certain issues.

"Frazier urged us along to discover the tea service for ourselves . . . tall glasses, set in braided jackets, to which loops of string were attached so that the glasses could be carried like pails."

Unit II
Design of Things
(Chapters 4-7)

The group begins its tour. The purpose of this unit is to show how the physical environment influences behavior. It demonstrates that improvements in equipment design and effective use of the landscape can increase job success and enhance living conditions.

Summary

The group enters a well-lit passageway with flowers and exciting paintings. When Frazier says that they will examine the paintings tomorrow, Burris slows his pace and begins to study them at length.

Burris finds himself separated from the others, seated on a bench next to a charming young woman. For several minutes he is surrounded by pleasant, well-mannered people, perfectly candid and lively. They are not effusive but clearly affectionate.

He regards them as people from another world. Not even certain they are speaking his language, suddenly he is afraid. With effort, he separates himself and finds his touring group.

Upon his return, Burris is introduced to Mrs. Meyerson, who informs the visitors about her special interest, women's clothing. She offers the group some tea, and at this point Frazier begins to discuss domestic engineering. At Walden Two everyone is encouraged to have a constantly experimental attitude, and improvements are sought in all spheres, including domestic life.

The tea service is not cups and saucers but rather tall, thin glasses. Set into braided straw jackets with loops of string for handles, they can be carried like pails. This domestic engineering prevents spilling, allows for an ample serving, and emphasizes odor and flavor. The glasses are pleasant and very light.

The bread-and-butter dishes are also made of thin glass. They are deep to prevent spilling, square for easy management, and with one edge rolled under to allow for a firm grip.

Frazier's explanations of domestic engineering evoke a mixed reaction. Burris is interested and Castle contemptuous. (Chapter 4)

Burris is struck by the many beautiful women in Walden Two, but Frazier asserts that the founders tried to obtain a representative sample of people. Personal appearance was not a factor in selection. Instead, many of the women appear beautiful because they are not restricted by contemporary styles. Walden Two tastes are broader than those in contemporary American society. Variety is encouraged, especially to accommodate individuals, and the chosen clothes often involve the least change, as in suits, sweaters, and skirts.

While talking with his guests, Frazier is interrupted by a group of children going to a birthday party. Seven-year-old Deborah is celebrating this event in the main dining room. As Frazier explains, at age seven children make the transition from their own dining facility to the main dining hall.

After the children have passed, Burris returns to their earlier conversation, noting that the men at Walden Two do not dress quite as well as the women. Frazier agrees and explains that this difference is due to American culture in general, in which men typically have been less concerned about clothes.

Near the top of the Ladder, the children continue to celebrate Deborah's birthday. Frazier stands aside, alone and unnoticed during the singing. Burris notes on his face an expression of deep feeling and perhaps even a tear. (Chapter 5)

Approaching the dining room, the guests stroll along "The Walk," a large corridor running the length of the main building. Burris remarks on the lack of crowds, and Frazier, in response, discusses cultural engineering. The staggered schedules for work, recreation, and dining in Walden Two allow the community to operate with minimal equipment and to enjoy a crowd-free environment.

An unusually popular movie or other performance is repeated until everyone has had a chance to see it. In the absence of advertising, the community's tastes vary, another reason for the lack of crowds. The staggered schedule also avoids crowds at the dining halls, bathrooms, businesses, and entertainment. With no institutional atmosphere, the days have flexibility and diversity. (Chapter 6)

Upon entering the dining hall, the group encounters more examples of domestic engineering. The dining rooms show a variety of styles, ranging from white-walled efficiency to a colorful Swedish room with a leisurely atmosphere. Burris is offended by this hodge-podge design and Frazier explains that, as another bit of cultural engineering, it helps the children adapt more readily to the unusual interiors encountered outside the community. Furthermore, Frazier adds vaguely, the development of aesthetic preferences occurs partly through associations with food.

Cultural engineering is evident throughout the dining hall. Mail deliveries are conveniently made to the compartments holding cloth napkins for everyone; the cabinets for silverware and condiments are adjacent; dinner trays are elliptical in shape for better use of space, and they have declivities for utensils and cups. These trays are also transparent, saving time for the dishwasher.

When Castle snorts at the latter detail, Frazier invites him to turn over a tray one thousand times, reminding his listeners that one of them would be compelled to do so in Walden Two if the trays were opaque. In contemporary American life, restaurants and hotels may have some industrialized housewifery, he points out, but it is generally not available to individual citizens. Furthermore, established tastes prevent restaurants from using some of these devices, such as the glass trays. (Chapter 7)

Key Concepts

Write a definition for each of these terms. When in doubt, reread the indicated pages in *Walden Two* and consult the glossary in this guidebook.

domestic engineering, 25

experimental attitude, 25

representative sample, 28

cultural engineering, 38

industrializing housewifery, 43

cooperative living, 43

Illustrations

The concepts in *Walden Two* are often illustrated in daily life. Below are students' illustrations of three concepts in this unit. Supply additional examples yourself of these or other key concepts in this unit.

�֎

Cultural engineering (38). "When I first visited my brother in California, he asked if there were anything special I would like to see or do. I answered, 'Yes! _____ land!' But I was in no way prepared for the type of experience we would have. I had imagined a sort of super amusement park where there would be huge crowds, lots of waiting in line, the necessity for keeping a close guard on one's pocketbook, hassles with reservations, parking and all the rest. Instead, it was like visiting another country where people behaved according to different laws and codes of ethics!

"Parking was easy, and no sooner had we gotten out of the car than a shuttle car stopped to take us into _____ land. As we were being seated, a voice from an overhead speaker told us where the shuttle would be stopping, and answered every question we might have thought of asking.

"We were free to get off at any stop we chose, and each one seemed more attractive than the one before. We selected our rides and shows at random since we could always change our minds.

"There were lots of people, but no crowds. Everyone was very friendly. We often found ourselves engaging in conversation with strangers. I soon relaxed about my pocketbook and everything else. I love the anthropomorphized critters. While I was there I absolutely believed they were real! It was possible to forget all about the outside world.

"We participated whole-heartedly in this society; we behaved as everyone else was behaving, and loved every minute of it. I believe I even smoked fewer cigarettes that day."

✖

Industrializing housewifery (43). "When I was in the third or fourth grade, a lady next door proposed that all neighbors make a day trip to an orchard and pick apples. Most people thought that it was a wonderful idea, but mothers with infants were hesitant. They were not sure that they would be free from their babies at any time during the trip. Their skepticism was not without a reason because they spent most of their days taking care of their babies. However, they ended up coming along, thinking some fresh air and different scenery would still be worthwhile. Of course, they brought their infants with them.

"Once arrived at the orchard, one of them came up with a 'brilliant' idea. A couple of them would watch all the babies while others would pick apples. The parents would take turns watching the infants, and during one's assigned time, the watcher would even feed them and change diapers. So, with a sense of freedom from their endless duties and of satisfaction about their ingenious arrangement, the young parents were able to pick as many apples as they could carry home."

✖

Cooperative living (43). "For the past six years I have been a member of a community food co-operative. The basis of this co-op is that everyone contributes some 'labor credits' to the farmwork.

"We have a group of planners, who decide on what foods we will cultivate, how to do so, and so forth. Even these people do some of the physical labor, in office or out of office, and of course they don't receive money. Everyone who works receives labor credits.

"Nobody is special or separate. Everybody is part of the general membership of the co-op. We are all our own employees, including the planners, at least when they are in the field. The planners make sure the jobs are rotated, so everyone does all kinds of work. They also ensure that members with special abilities have the chance to use them, for these are valuable to the whole co-op. The outcome for everyone is fresh, organic food at a very low cost.

"Most of the members are quite pleased with their work, which contributes directly to earning a living. Each member can also contribute suggestions to the planners for improving the co-op. Most of us seem quite happy with our jobs and even contribute more than the necessary labor credits. I think part of this is the result of the friendships among the members. The common, obviously important activity develops a strong community spirit."

Study Questions

1. Describe the Walden Two tea service. How are the citizens of Walden Two encouraged to view all habits and customs? How would you improve our contemporary cafeteria services, suitcases, health practices, bathrooms, clothing, or classroom? (25)

2. What is the approach to fashion in Walden Two? Frazier says people must broaden their tastes. Do you agree? What would be the implications for consumers? (28)

3. When does "full dress" occur in Walden Two? How might this custom increase or decrease happiness? (30)

4. What does Frazier do at the child's birthday? What does this reaction suggest about his thoughts? About him? (33)

5. Compare the Walk and the Ladder. How are they similar in construction and purpose? How are they different? (34, 20)

6. What is Frazier's view of crowds? In what ways, if any, is he correct? Incorrect? (35, 37)

7. How is the lecture viewed in Walden Two? Should it have any place in contemporary higher education? (36)

8. Describe the Walden Two staggered schedule. What are its advantages? Disadvantages? (38)

9. Describe the posters in the serving room of the dining hall. In what ways, if any, are they concerned with education, experimentation, and socialization? (41)

10. Indicate the chief feature of the dining room trays. Give your opinion of the advantages and disadvantages for utility and attractiveness. (42)

Values Clarification

Castle emerges as the most dissident visitor, asking for explanations of many Walden Two practices. Frazier speaks on the following topics:

1. On experiments: "A constantly experimental attitude toward everything—that's all we need." (25)

2. On dress codes: "Full dress is a form of conspicuous consumption which doesn't amuse us—except when we see it in others." (30)

3. On crowds: "But why should anyone who isn't starved for friendship or affection enjoy a crowd?" (35)

4. On public speaking: "We solve the problem of the lecturer by dispensing with him." (36)

Indicate the order of these topics, 1st through 4th, according to their importance for you, apart from Frazier's views. If necessary, use the page number to reread these passages.

Think about Frazier's comments. Did they influence your ranking? If so, how? Then prepare a brief essay defending your ranking.

This process, values clarification, enables people to attain greater insight into their attitudes and opinions. It also promotes understanding of their priorities among issues in modern life.

"We were to wash all the south windows of the main building, beginning at the west end. In an attempt to get into the spirit of 'industrialized housewifery,' we organized ourselves. . . ."

Unit III
Working, Playing
(Chapters 8-11)

The touring group acquires labor credits. The purpose of this unit is to consider the nature and role of work in modern life. There should be dignity in all work; it should be distributed among all citizens; a leisure class, if permitted, will make increasing demands on others; with proper efficiency, planning, and control, no one need work more than half the typical working day in modern society.

Summary

After dinner, Burris thanks Frazier for his hospitality. Frazier explains that it is no imposition for him. He earns labor credits for taking charge of their visit.

Labor credits serve as currency in Walden Two. All goods and services are free; each member contributes to the community with twelve hundred labor credits each year. The number of labor credits required from each member depends upon the needs of the community. In its present state, members of Walden Two work only four hours a day.

As Frazier explains, different credit values are assigned to different types of work. The less pleasant the work, the higher is its credit value. A man in a sewer needs to work only two hours per day. The credit value for working with flowers is so low that no one can make a living simply by working in the flower garden.

Castle resists the idea of labor credits, suggesting that Walden Two does not offer complete freedom of choice in work. Frazier replies that, with so many attractive alternatives, no one is unhappy if a particular course of action is not available. There are many others. It is the same way with the choice of a mate, he replies. The idea of "one and only" arises more from singleness of opportunity than from constancy of the heart.

This statement provokes Burris to inquire about the government of Walden Two. The only government, Frazier explains, is a Board of Planners, three men and three women, who may serve up to ten years. These Planners are responsible for the overall state of the community. They make policy, review the success of the Managers, and have judicial functions. They receive two labor credits per day, and of the two remaining labor credits, one must be physical labor.

The Managers, as the name implies, are in charge of specific services. Thus, there are Managers of Health, Arts, Food, Dentistry, Play, the Nursery School, and others. They have an immediate, direct concern for specific functions in the community, and they are the hardest workers.

The community members neither choose nor elect Planners or Managers. But, according to Frazier, they do not want a voice in the matter, anyway. Community members may become trained and tested as Managers, if they wish, through apprenticeships and intermediate positions, and then the Managers, in turn, make nominations for the Board of Planners, which selects its own replacements.

To eliminate the caste system, there are no honorific titles. For example, Mr. Meyerson is a certified doctor and Worker. Furthermore, there are only Planners, Managers, and Workers, apart from the Scientists, who deal with practical problems and, like Managers, receive two or three labor credits per day.

Both brains and brawn are required by everyone in the labor force. Everyone does one or two hours of physical work each day, which keeps the community healthy and ensures that the Planners, Managers and Scientists will not forget the problems of the big-muscle user.

Most striking to Castle and Burris is the four-hour workday. Frazier cites seven reasons why Walden Two can operate in this manner.. First, people work more quickly and skillfully because the fatigue factor is less. Second, they produce more because motivation is high; they are working for their community, not for a profit-taking boss. Third, everyone in the community contributes; there is no unemployment. Fourth, there is better use of workers. Everyone works with the best labor-serving devices, the most efficient methods, and appropriate training. Fifth, Walden Two has eliminated unnecessary jobs: banks, loan companies, advertising agencies, insurance businesses, funeral parlors, bars, taverns, and so forth. Sixth, Walden Two has doubled its workforce by fully employing women, and they also use industrialized housewifery. Seventh, there is a low consumption of goods, despite the high standard of living. Personal wealth is small. The members, practicing the Thoreauvian principle, avoid unnecessary possessions.

Before the visitors retire to their rooms, Frazier indicates that they too will be expected to contribute labor credits. Otherwise, he explains, the members of Walden Two would feel inhospitable, for their guests would be thinking that they ought to leave. (Chapter 8)

The next morning after breakfast the guests proceed to the Work Desk to choose their jobs for earning labor credits. They decide to wash windows at one point two credits. For efficiency, they organize themselves into three pairs and divide the job into three parts: removing, cleaning, and polishing the windows. At the end of the two-hour period, Burris decides that this work is better than grading blue books, and a red-faced Castle rates it higher than reading term papers. (Chapter 9)

During lunch Frazier compares Walden Two with other self-sufficient communities returning to primitive modes of farming and industry. Walden Two goes to the farm for food and clothing, but it does not ignore technology. The community is interested in saving labor. The aim is to diminish the work, not the worker.

A truck ride after lunch takes the visitors to the dairy, where the Dairy Manager describes the work with milk, cream, fodder, and manure. Burris notes a difference between the Manager and Frazier in the way they regard the farm equipment. For the Manager, a cream separator extracts the cream. For Frazier, it saves labor and time. The Manager is concerned with the specifics of each job; Frazier is concerned with general principles and social engineering.

With pride, Frazier explains how social engineering aided the farmers, who were being ostracized due to the objectionable odors they acquired from their work. A building was divided into three parts: a room for dress clothes, a shower room, and a room for work clothes. Coming to work, the farmers took off their dress clothes, took a shower, and changed into work clothes. Leaving work, they used these rooms in the reverse order for the opposite purpose.

While the guests visit a series of workshops, Frazier explains that the community is not completely self-sufficient. There is a "foreign exchange," not yet entirely satisfactory. Frazier feels it could be more efficient.

They visit buildings for looms, woodworking, and metal-working, as well as experimental laboratories and a shed with an earth-rammer, at which most of the workers are surprisingly young. Frazier explains that they are probably building their own living quarters. He refers to this interest as "a sort of nesting instinct," part of being in love in the community.

In the clothing shop, Mary demonstrates an unusual stitch on a large embroidery frame, and her contribution is appreciated by members of the community. No one thanks her, and fortunately Mary expected no direct expression, which would have made everyone uneasy. (Chapter 10)

Before dinner, Burris examines the bulletin board, which has announcements for meetings, parties, concerts, and other entertainment. Frazier points out that the community does not need garish posters. Simple notices are quite sufficient because the community members have been conditioned to be excited by these posters. They evoke the pleasant experiences which they have preceded in the past.

Concerts at Walden Two generally are fifty minutes long. The ease with which community members can attend them makes fifty minutes appropriate. In the city, the trip to the concert, parking, buying the tickets, perhaps bad weather, and the other miscellaneous tasks require a two- or three-hour performance. For all the time and effort involved, a shorter performance would not be satisfactory.

Frazier directs the conversation towards patronage of the arts. Why, he asks, is the American culture so lacking in production of art, compared with science and technology? The answer is because the proper conditions are not available.

"Prizes," Frazier stresses, "only scratch the surface. You can't encourage art with money alone."

Artists must be free from the responsibility of earning a livelihood in order to produce their works. This is the essence of art—it draws on energies and talents which, under more demanding circumstances, would go into earning a livelihood. In addition, artists need more social support; they need to be stimulated and appreciated.

Cultural engineering at Walden Two attempts to give each person the opportunity to develop as far as possible in a given area. The environment is arranged to provide suitable resources and an appreciative audience. Children are exposed to opportunities in music and art in their earliest years.

Burris objects: "How many geniuses can you expect to get from a limited assortment of genes?" A discussion of the roles of heredity and environment ensues with Burris arguing for the former and Frazier for the latter. Whatever the answer, Frazier says, we must make the most of our genes by establishing the most favorable environments. At this point Burris remembers the impressive paintings in the Ladder. All of them, says Frazier, were painted by members of the community. "Right conditions, that's all," he says. "Right conditions. . . ."

Burris ruminates on the psychology of artistic creation and decides that he should research that area in the library. Then he realizes how differently Frazier would approach the problem. The answer for Frazier would not be in books but in experimentation.

In the final scene, Frazier, Castle, and Burris enjoy a small concert. They are most impressed, especially Burris. (Chapter 11)

Key Concepts

Write a definition for each of these terms. When in doubt, reread the indicated pages in *Walden Two* and consult the glossary in this guidebook.

labor credits, 45

Planners, 48

Managers, 48

social engineering, 71

conditioned reflex, 77

Philistinism, 78

Illustrations

The concepts in *Walden Two* are often illustrated in daily life. Below are students' illustrations of three concepts in this unit. Supply additional examples yourself of these or other key concepts in this unit.

Labor credits (45). "Our family unit has operated over the past 23 years somewhat on the labor credit principle. All services were free to family members. There were of course different providers of different services. Actual entries were not made in ledgers, but the chores were always being evaluated and willingness levels changed.

"For example, bringing in wood in the fall was an eagerly awaited chore when we were children, but now that we are young adults the willingness level of that chore has changed dramatically. That chore would have been rated about a .4, but now it is a definite 2.

"A chore that my father, my two older sisters and I all hate is going to the dump. We all rate that as a solid 2. But my 16-year-old sister rates that as .6. It's another excuse for her to drive all over town! Past history shows that the willingness level of that chore changes at about age 17."

Social engineering (71). "After graduating from high school, I worked in a fast-food store for several years and gradually worked my way up to a supervisory position. I was in charge of about 10 to 12 college students, and it was my job to train them and then keep them happy and productive in their work.

"I got some of my ideas from watching supervisors in businesses all over town. In one supermarket where I often shopped, the head guy was on everyone's back all the time—telling baggers to hurry up, checking on the cashiers, and asking why shelves weren't stocked, always with a negative, critical tone. Most of the employees worked hard, or pretended to work, when this manager was around, but they quit as soon as he disappeared. He was dictatorial and people worked only for that reason. They certainly didn't care about him, the store, or even the customers.

"In a restaurant across town things were very different. This place was a combined restaurant and deli, and the guy in charge, sort of a head waiter and counter manager, ignored the other employees completely, and so they stood around and just gabbed while customers needed water, menus, or their orders. They even overlooked customers trying to get their attention. The whole approach was laissez-faire and nobody was happy—not the waiters, not the customers, not even the head waiter himself. After some months, that place changed ownership.

"I decided to try the obvious third approach—paying attention to my workers, giving plenty of support. For each new person, I explained the goals of the fast-food service and the particular contribution the new person would make. Then I trained that person as fully as possible, pointing out how each part of the training contributed to the overall goal. And then I tried to stay off their backs. Instead, I let them know when they did a good job and tried to keep motivation as high as possible.

"Part of the success, I discovered, was to let the workers make some of the decisions themselves, making them feel responsibility for the overall success of the business. Some of them actually seemed to enjoy the work quite a bit, trying to increase their speed, find new ways to put on the condiments, and so forth. I really think our customers enjoyed coming in partly due to the obvious team spirit among our work crews, all because I tried to accent the positive and not ignore anyone."

Conditioned reflex (77). "My mother, with six kids, was a busy woman, and one of us was always sick. For the sake of efficiency, she always put a big green garbage bag at the head of the sick child's bed—for refuse of all sorts, including handkerchiefs, bandages, and medicine bottles, and even in case we had to vomit.

"After several illnesses, once with the measles I remember in particular, I began to associate those bags with feeling awful. And then I discovered I felt queasy just bringing the bag to my mom for use with one of my brothers. It was a conditioned reaction, certainly, for I was not sick at all.

"But that was long ago and since I've been married that reaction has changed. My husband uses these bags for leaves and then bonfires, for we live out in the country. I love the smell of the leaves burning, and I enjoy frolicking with Jim in the process. My earlier sensation actually has been replaced by a very slight but pleasant glow on seeing the bags, at least in the fall."

Study Questions

1. Describe the Walden Two system of labor credits. Does it seem desirable? Does it seem possible? (45)

2. Compare the Board of Planners and the Board of Managers. What are their special functions? (48)

3. "But four hours a day!" Castle exclaims. "I can't take that seriously." Then Frazier describes a half-dozen methods for decreasing the workday from eight hours to four. What are they? Do they seem feasible? (52-56)

4. Describe the place where farmers prepare for work. Why has it decreased labor credits for farming? Is it an example of social engineering? Why or why not? (71)

5. Is Walden Two completely self-sufficient? What problems does this situation pose for establishing a larger Walden Two or many such societies? (72)

6. Inspecting the work areas, the touring group goes from cloth-making, woodworking, metalworking, and a machine shop to some experimental laboratories. What might be going on in the laboratories? Cite some specific examples. Indicate their relevance for Walden Two. (73-74)

7. How long are the programs of entertainment in Walden Two? In modern urban society, they are two or three hours. What is Frazier's explanation of the difference? Do you agree or disagree? Why? (78)

8. What is the Walden Two view on cultivation of the arts? Does it seem feasible? Are there comparable opportunities in modern society? If so, what are they? (80)

9. Frazier says our civilization is running away with itself: "Problems are born faster than they can be solved." What does he mean? Give an example. (81)

10. Walden Two purportedly will achieve "a Golden Age" in the arts. Why? Explain Frazier's position with reference to the heredity-environment issue in musical families. (83)

Values Clarification

The group visits the work areas, including the storehouses, farm, and shops. Frazier becomes even more candid:

1. On choosing a mate: "The tender sentiment of the 'one and only' has less to do with constancy of heart than with singleness of opportunity." (47)

2. On physicians: "The medical profession has been slow to give up the chicanery of prescientific medicine." (49)

3. On physical labor: "We mustn't let our big muscles atrophy just because we've devised superior ways of using the little ones." (52)

4. On artists: "Artists aren't lazy, but they must be reasonably free of the responsibility of earning a livelihood." (80)

What is your opinion of his remarks? Write "NOW" beside the comment with which you agree most, the comment which seems most sensible to you.

Consider these same remarks from your perspective two or three years ago. Write "THEN" beside the comment which you would have considered most sensible at that time.

Since human beings are always in the process of development, your two choices perhaps differ. If so, speculate on the possible reasons. In your presentation, show how these factors may be more or less influential at different times in your life.

"' . . . at such an early age the problem of not licking the lollipop isn't easy. Now what would you do, Mr. Castle, in a similar situation?'"

Unit IV
Raising Children
(Chapters 12-15)

Childrearing should proceed according to the child's readiness in each realm: emotional, motivational, social, intellectual, and physical. This unit shows that if children are to develop to the fullest, growth rates must be considered carefully and the environment planned accordingly.

Summary

The six visitors spend the morning visiting the community nurseries and schools. They begin in the Lower Nursery, where all the children are infants in their first year. A white-uniformed Mrs. Nash is in charge.

Each baby, in a separate cubicle with a large glass window, wears only diapers, and there are no bedclothes. The air is filtered and temperature controlled, and each cubicle is fairly soundproof. The result is little or no laundry for bedclothes or diapers; there is protection against disease; the infants need to be bathed only once a week; and they do not awaken one another.

"Looks like an aquarium," sneers Castle.

Mrs. Nash explains that the proper temperature for a newborn is 88 to 90 degrees. At six months it is 80 degrees. This information has been obtained by observing the babies carefully.

"Controlled temperature, noiseless sleep–aren't these babies going to be completely at the mercy of a normal environment?" Castle asks. "Can you go on coddling them forever?"

Annoyances are introduced slowly, Mrs. Nash continues, depending upon the capacity of the baby to tolerate them. The procedure is much like inoculation.

"What about mother love?" Castle asks.

Frazier points out that mother's love, father's love, all sorts of love are supplied in liberal doses. It is not marred, he says, by coming from someone who is overworked or ignorant about childrearing. (Chapter 12)

❦❦❦❦

In the Upper Nursery, the children are 1 to 3 years old, amid Lilliputian furniture. Since the environment is again temperature-controlled and humidity-controlled, they sleep in diapers without bedclothes. At play, most are naked; a few wear training pants.

The discussion turns to frustration and jealousy. Frazier explains that these emotions are almost unknown in Walden Two.

"But emotions are—fun!" Barbara objects.

Some of them are productive, Frazier agrees, such as the strengthening powers of joy and love. But the high-voltage excitements of anger and fear are not necessary in modern life. These negative emotions, once useful in the evolution of the human species, are now wasteful and destructive, even jealousy, which is a minor form of anger.

When a particular emotion is no longer useful, we eliminate it, Frazier explains. "It's simply a matter of behavioral engineering."

At this point, the group wants to understand behavioral engineering and Frazier, with a shrug of his shoulders, guides everyone to the shade of a large tree. Here they await his discourse on this important topic. (Chapter 13)

🌿🦌 🦌🌿

In the early phases, Frazier worked with a young Planner named Simmons, studying all the great literary works on morals and ethics, searching for methods of imparting self-control. The chief suggestions, however, came from clinical psychology: building tolerance for annoying situations by administering them in small doses, according to the individual's readiness. The process is like immunization.

In a lesson on dealing with frustration, subclass A_3, administered at age 3 or 4 years, the child receives a powdered lollipop which can be eaten later in the day, if it is not licked earlier. The children are helped with solutions: first putting the candy out of sight, then playing games, and later even examining their own reactions.

At a later age, the problem is made still more difficult. The lollipop is hung around each child's neck. The idea is to administer the lessons in carefully graded sequences, rather than accidental dosages. Burris objects, however, that jealousy and envy cannot be administered in graded doses.

"And why not?" asks Frazier. "Remember we control the social environment too at this age."

In the Forbidden Soup lesson, the children arrive for supper, tired and hungry, and find they must wait five minutes in front of their steaming bowls of soup. Their task is to avoid unhappiness, which they learn to do by making jokes and singing songs, as easily as we might tolerate a five-minute delay at curtain time.

Later, when an appropriate level of readiness has been reached, jokes and games are not permitted. The children must wait in silence, forced back upon their own resources.

Later still, they must deal with envy or jealousy. Each child is designated "heads" or "tails," a coin is flipped, and the winners dine while the losers wait another five minutes.

Again, the basic concern is readiness. The children are confronted with a series of gradually increasing annoyances, appropriate to their capacity to manage them. If there is resentment in the forbidden soup, it is directed against Lady Luck, against the coin toss, not against the lucky diners.

"I must say," Castle protests, "I think you and your friend Simmons are really very subtle sadists."

Frazier points out that earlier Castle accused him of breeding "softies," and now he objects to tougher procedures. The point, he insists, is that these challenging situations are never very difficult because of the careful schedules.

Castle claims that these methods rob the children of motivation. They take the spring from the watch, he says.

"That's an experimental question, Mr. Castle, and you have the wrong answer," Frazier replies.

30

"Would you relax control of the environment and let the child meet accidental frustrations?" he continues. *"But what is the virtue of accident?* No, there was only one course open to us. We had to *design* a series of adversities so that the child would develop the greatest possible self-control." (Chapter 14)

The living quarters and daily schedules of the older children show further evidence of behavioral engineering. When younger, they progressed from an air-conditioned cubicle to an air-conditioned room and then to a cot in a dormitory. Now, at age 5 or 6, they live in separate living alcoves in groups of three and four. After another year or two, they will move into small rooms until the early teens, with frequent changes of roommates providing a variety of living experiences. At age 13, like adults, they become eligible for the larger, single rooms.

The group then tours the educational environment: laboratories, studies, workshops, and reading rooms, typically used in place of classrooms. Many of the instructors are men, and it is not even clear that the children are in school. The emphasis is not on traditional school subjects; it is on techniques of learning and thinking.

The touring group returns to the shade of their large tree. The school is family and vice versa, Frazier explains, with no emphasis on grade levels. The grade is an administrative device which disrupts the child's developmental process. In Walden Two the child advances according to his readiness, with no distinction between grade school, high school, or college.

The library keeps only the most up-to-date, useful books. Two or three thousand volumes are sufficient.

In the absence of low grades, expulsion, honors, diplomas, and so forth, Castle wants to know what is done about the standard motives for learning. What makes the child want to learn?

"We made a survey of the motives of the unhampered child and found more than we could use," replies Frazier. "Our engineering job was to *preserve* them by fortifying the child against discouragement."

Discouragement is introduced as carefully and gradually as other adverse experiences, beginning around six months of age. Even the toys are designed for this purpose. The child pulls on a toy ring, producing a bit of a tune or a pattern of flashing lights. Later, the child must pull twice, then thrice, and then several times before the result is forthcoming, thereby developing a high degree of persistence.

The motives in education, Frazier explains, are the same as those in all human behavior, a drive to control the environment. It makes the baby crumple and recrumple a piece of noisy paper; it makes the scientist press forward with research. Properly trained, or properly shielded from inappropriate events early in life, people do not need extrinsic rewards and punishments.

Castle complains that the Walden Two citizens will be too happy to be creative. On the contrary, Frazier replies, when the necessities and frustrations of life are satisfied, artistic interests will flourish, as will inborn differences. With no barriers to educational and cultural opportunities, each child will develop in its most appropriate ways, resulting in a broad range of talents and interests in the total population. (Chapter 15)

Key Concepts

Write a definition for each of these terms. When in doubt, reread the indicated pages in *Walden Two* and consult the glossary in this guidebook.

tolerance for frustration, 88

community love, 90

"self-control," 96

experimental question, 103

design a series of adversities, 105

environment, 107

Illustrations

The concepts in *Walden Two* are often illustrated in daily life. Below are students' illustrations of three concepts in this unit. Supply additional examples yourself of these or other key concepts in this unit.

"Self-control" (96). "In any fancy shop, especially a clothing store, my older sister knows no bounds. She just goes wild. A new fall shirt is on display and she just must have it. It will go so well with her such-and-such sweater, a certain necklace, her shoes, or whatever. And out comes her magic card—the plastic money which you never have, never seem to spend.

"The ads today all count on our need for instant gratification: 'You can have it all.' So people go out and spend a lot of time and a lot of money they don't really have for things they don't really need. I think people today, in their twenties particularly, could have used some early temptation training with soup or coins or whatever. Give 'em lollipop lessons. They need help to ignore the enticements of our massive credit-card society, surely temptation's 'trump card.'"

Experimental question (103). "A number of weeks ago, my husband and I did an experiment wherein we did not turn on our television set for 7 days. The aim of the experiment was to answer this question: How would we spend our leisure time if we did not watch television? And would we enjoy these television-less days?

"After the 7 days we had both completed several projects which had previously been put off because 'there just aren't enough hours in the day.' We also read more and talked more to each other than during a t.v. filled week.

"As a result of this experiment we now enjoy several t.v.-less days per week. We are also contemplating an experiment with certain foods and living without a pet."

Design a series of adversities (105). "I never gave my mother credit for being particularly creative or enlightened in child-rearing techniques. As I reflect back though I can recollect a very good use of behavioral techniques. Two swimming instructors had given up in their attempts to get me to put my face in the water. It seemed as though I was a child who would never learn to swim. Finally my mother decided that she would work with me.

"We went to the shallow end of the pool and she threw my favorite toy in the water. It sank. Without hesitation I retrieved the toy and eagerly returned it to her for another dunking. She threw it in the water again but just a little further out. I had to actually get my elbows wet. This wasn't exactly comfortable but I was having too much fun to stop. The next toss was in water deep enough that I had to actually get my shoulder wet. The process was repeated until I was comfortable at each successive depth. The next toss required that my neck and part of my cheek get wet and the game continued at that level. The next toss was just deep enough that I had to place my entire face in the water. Without instruction on 'breath-holding techniques' I plunged to the bottom, retrieved my toy and didn't realize that she had done in one hour what swimming instructors couldn't do in two previous weeks."

Study Questions

1. According to Mrs. Nash, what is the proper temperature for a newborn baby? How does she know? Could this same technique be used with animals? (87)

2. Frazier and Castle fall into a dispute about mother love. What are their views? What is your conception of mother love? How does it compare with Frazier's father love and everybody's love? (89)

3. Frazier says: "When a particular emotion is no longer a useful part of a behavioral repertoire, we proceed to eliminate it." In Walden Two, how do they do so? (93)

4. During a dispute about environmental control in the nurseries, Frazier says to Castle: "A while ago you accused me of breeding a race of softies. Now you object to toughening them up." What is Frazier's point here? In your answer, refer to his comment about the virtue of accident. (102)

5. Frazier and Castle have a heated discussion about childrearing. As children, did they wear a lollipop or face a bowl of forbidden soup? What is the point here about Frazier and Castle and childrearing? (106)

6. In Walden Two, what is the relation between home training and school training? Do you agree with this approach? Why? (109)

7. Describe the school grades and grade levels in Walden Two. What are the advantages and disadvantages? (109)

8. What is the Walden Two approach to library collections? What would your librarian say about it? And what would be the view of eminent scholars? (111)

9. Suppose a child is easily discouraged with his ability to play checkers. Describe a program, using Frazier's behavioral engineering, which would lead to greater pleasure and success on the part of the child. (114)

10. It is sometimes said that in a community like Walden Two everyone will be just alike. Why do people take this view? Does this outcome seem likely to you? Why? (117)

Values Clarification

Castle's resistance to the child-rearing practices is readily evident in the nurseries. Frazier retorts angrily, "You wouldn't understand, however, because you're not so far advanced as our children." In this same style, he adds:

1. On emotional development: "But sorrow and hate and the high-voltage excitements of anger, fear, and rage are out of proportion with the needs of modern life, and they're wasteful and dangerous." (92)

2. On self-control: "But don't be misled, the control always rests in the last analysis in the hands of society." (96)

3. On school grades: "The grade is an administrative device which does violence to the nature of the developmental process." (109)

4. On children's motives for learning: "Our engineering job was to preserve them by fortifying the child against discouragement." (114)

Place a check beside the remark which you would like most to discuss with Frazier. Remember that he is a social philosopher with a practical side, too.

In planning your discussion with him, focus on the importance of his remark for you. Show why it is especially important.

Consider briefly the solution or outcome Frazier desires. Reread the relevant passages, if necessary. Do you agree or disagree with Frazier? Why? Give primary attention, however, to the importance of the issue, not its solution.

"Just south of the flower gardens, on a blanket spread
out on the warm grass, lay a naked baby nine or ten
months old. A boy and girl were trying to make her crawl
toward a rubber doll."

Unit V
Marriage and the Family
(Chapters 16-18)

The age of Walden Two parents astonishes the visitors. This unit emphasizes adolescents' readiness for sex, the advantages of early marriage, and the assets of a community approach to child-rearing. The children, the biological parents, and childless couples all benefit from this practice. This unit also points to weaknesses in the nuclear family as an economic, social, and psychological institution.

Summary

En route to lunch, the visitors observe a boy and girl playing with a baby, and they are amazed to discover that the infant is the couple's child. At the birth of her first child, the average Walden Two mother is eighteen, Frazier explains, abruptly leaving his guests for a moment.

"It's a handy thing, this experimental attitude," muses Castle a bit sarcastically, thinking of the earlier discussion of child-rearing.

Later, at a small table in the English Inn, the conversation returns to early marriage. Frazier is the advocate, Castle the skeptic, and Burris the mediator.

Frazier's argument is that there is no economic obstacle to marriage at any age in Walden Two. All children are cared for in the same way, regardless of the parents' background. At fifteen or sixteen, girls are ready for childbearing, and at that age boys and girls have a capacity for love that they will never experience again. Adolescence, he points out, is seldom pleasant, and at Walden Two it is as brief and painless as possible.

Beginning childbearing early, many women at Walden Two are finished at age twenty-two or three. Adult life offers many interesting prospects, including the maternal role.

Burris suddenly realizes that a generation at Walden Two is twenty rather than the usual thirty years. A man can be a grandfather at thirty-five. Frazier enjoys Burris' astonishment and explains that the average member of Walden Two knows many more of his descendants than does someone in society at large.

Statistics, Barbara argues, show that early marriages are unhappy. Frazier replies that they fail because of economic hardship, which is unknown at Walden Two. Furthermore, when a couple becomes engaged, they visit the Manager of Marriages, who advises against a marriage with any great discrepancy between the pair in intellectual ability or temperament. The boys and girls at Walden Two also know each other very well. Early marriage in Walden Two shortens adolescence and allows the couple to enjoy the subsequent years.

At this point, Burris asks about human genetic experiments. Frazier replies that there are none at present but experimental breeding may become possible with the weakening of family structure. (Chapter 16)

Frazier considers the family. He explains that the decline of the family is the most significant story in the history of our times. The Walden Two community replaces the family, an ancient institution which is out of place in a society not based on blood ties. The home has declined as a medium for perpetuating culture, and Walden Two has dealt with the economic, social, and psychological bases of the problem. Experimentation continues at Walden Two with regard to family practices.

In one instance, some husbands and wives agreed to live alone or in pairs, depending upon random assignments, and the results showed that couples with separate rooms were happier than couples sharing a room. In terms of health, convenience, and personal freedom, two rooms served better than one. Loyalty and affection also seemed to be greater when each person had his or her own room.

"Free love" is not practiced at Walden Two, but "free affection" is common. If a marital bond is weakened or broken, for one reason or another, the individuals rarely feel deserted.

Frazier admits that extramarital friendships may weaken the marital tie. Then a psychologist gives counsel, leading to readjustment or possibly divorce.

Burris argues that group child care may weaken the parent-child bond. Frazier agrees that it does, partly by design, but for the child group care is better than parental care. Traditional parents often do not know the basic principles of child-rearing. Furthermore, the home is not the place to raise children, even when the parents know what to do. There are too many distractions and dangers for the child.

Group care is also an advantage for adults. The biological parents are relieved of a large responsibility and many household duties. Instead, they can visit their children, working and playing with them, whenever they wish. They have less concern about divorce, for the children are not disrupted, and adults for whom parenthood is inappropriate find no stigma attached. Finally, there is an advantage for childless couples, who can participate in the child-rearing process.

"Don't these attenuated personal ties lead to feelings of insecurity?" asks Castle.

"Who is insecure?" asks Frazier. "Not our children, certainly." Then he enumerates several more advantages for children.

Around the children are a number of adults, rather than a single parent, creating numerous possibilities for a suitable identification. Furthermore, these adults are both men and women; there is no problem of unbalanced relations with the sexes. Most important, since the caretakers are not overworked, emotional, or unprepared, the children have an increased feeling of security in the group context. (Chapter 17)

Finished with this discussion of child-rearing, the visitors report to the Work Desk. Castle and the women earn their labor credits by some unspecified work while Rodge, Steve, and Burris choose to stack wood.

During their work, Rodge appeals to Burris for advice. He would like to join Walden Two but feels that Barbara would not agree. During their visit, he has decided that Barbara is not particularly concerned with social issues but rather with having a home, a car, and entertaining her friends. He decides that Barbara has changed, but Burris says, "I think you've done the changing, Rodge." (Chapter 18)

Key Concepts

Write a definition for each of these terms. When in doubt, reread the indicated pages in *Walden Two* and consult the glossary in this guidebook.

sex problem, 121

family, 128

free affection, 129

prescientific days, 131

identification, 134

social conscience, 140

Illustrations

The concepts in *Walden Two* are often illustrated in daily life. Below are students' illustrations of three concepts in this unit. Supply additional examples yourself of these or other key concepts in this unit.

❦

Free affection (129). "In my first high school, in another part of the country, nobody ever hugged anybody. Nobody held anyone, either. There was just no touching at all in public. In fact, if you touched or slightly bumped someone in the elevator, you quickly pulled away and said, 'Excuse me!'

"My family moved and I entered _____ Alternative School here, to try something new. On my first day I was astonished when students and faculty went up and hugged each other all day, asking about summer vacations, greeting each other so warmly. I felt quite alone, for I knew no one and nobody hugged me—and anyway I wasn't sure I wanted to be hugged that way, at least at that particular time.

"It seemed I just didn't belong. Of course, no one really noticed that I didn't hug anybody.

"I thought the next day things would be different. They were—but only slightly. No more 'How-was-your-summer?' greetings, but people still hugged and touched regularly, and a girl I had met earlier casually patted me on the shoulder after a short chat.

"From that moment on my stiffness began to leave me. I began to make friends with teachers as well as students, and they would make physical contact, usually touching my arm or holding my hand whenever we chatted. It was all just part of communicating, part of being a member of that community—and I quickly learned to enjoy it.

"I guess the term for this would be 'free affection' but no one ever even gave it a name. It was the way people were. People outside the school, especially some nosey and somewhat bigoted neighbors, thought of it as free sex, or free love, and _____ Alternate School had a very bad reputation with them. We were a bunch of degenerates, teachers included.

"Most of the students, in early adolescence, were dealing with new feelings and quite sensitive about relations with the opposite sex, what to do, and the approach in _____ School filled some of our needs for direct, physical contact. It was far superior to the first school, where there was no contact at all, except for the secret fumblings on dates. And, in fact, I think at _____ we were less active sexually, partly because we satisfied the need for touch, and recognized the difference between free affection and free love."

❦

Identification (134). "My mother makes a point of being extremely selfless, often to the point of false martyrdom. She will never eat the white meat of the chicken, even though she prefers it, because 'she has to leave enough for her husband and children.' My father often buys himself new books and records, but my mother refuses to buy herself things she would enjoy, like new clothes. She insists on making all her own clothes: 'We simply do not have enough money for me to indulge *myself*.'

"Her attitude often hurt me as a child because it seemed that everything I did was selfish in her eyes. She once told me, 'You will never be as good a mother as I am. You are too selfish. You will never sacrifice for your family as I do.' I remember feeling guilty even then for my supposed selfishness. Now her attitude annoys me because it often does not seem to be generously given.

"In recent years, however, I have noticed the same attitude in myself. I am too often submissive to others. Not wanting to be selfish, I often allow others to take precedence over me. I hesitate to choose something that I want if I think it differs from what my friend or boyfriend wants. My boyfriend has said to me occasionally, 'I wish you weren't always so selfless. You should think more of yourself and believe that your desires are important also.' I realize when he says this that I have taken this quality which I dislike in my mother and made it part of me, also."

✻❦✻

Social conscience (140). "It was 2:15 on a Tuesday morning during the summer. My two friends, Jacques and Sandy, and I had missed the 1:15 A.M. train back home and thus had an hour to kill in Penn Station with the citizens of a smelly hellhole. The guys wanted some orange juice so they took off in search of a 24-hour store while I massaged my aching feet.

"I was so involved in my task that at first I didn't notice 'John.' He was sitting 5 feet in front of me. His eyes had a faraway look, almost as if he was in a world that I couldn't enter. His reddish—brown hair was matted with dirt and lice and his clothes were torn and dirty. Next to his slumped body was a large plastic bag full of tin cans. I tried to erase his face from my memory as I started my other foot, but I kept visualizing his shoeless feet and empty expression. I wanted to do something, but I didn't know what. I glanced at him quickly again, hoping that he wouldn't notice. He turned and looked not at me but more through me as if I wasn't there. I felt the urge to ask him how his life had been reduced to a worn grey suit, an income of cans, and a bed of yesterday's *New York Times*. I was interrupted by the return of my friends who were rushing me because it was 3:10 A.M.

"I put on my shoes and started to walk away. I touched my purse. My fingers were ready to give John my last $5, yet I just kept walking. Suddenly, something snapped inside me and I stopped my friends and ran back to put a dollar by his feet. 'Not even a word of thanks,' I thought later. It didn't matter though because I was on a warm, clean train going home. But I couldn't forget that his home was the passenger waiting area of Penn Station."

✻❦✻

Study Questions

1. What is the Walden Two approach to sex among young adults? Does it seem wholesome? Reasonable? Possible? Practical? (122)

2. How long is a generation in Walden Two? What are the implications for population size? Family life? The elderly? (123)

3. Statistics suggest that early marriages in contemporary society tend to be unhappy. Frazier claims the opposite is true in Walden Two. For what reasons? How do you resolve the difference between the two societies? (124)

4. Describe the experiment on rooms for married couples. What was the procedure? The finding? Assuming the finding is correct, what complicating factors may be present? (129)

5. "Oh, Mother! I am so glad you brought a present just for me." Is this sentence likely to be uttered by a Walden Two child? If so, why? If not, why not? Indicate the background for your answer. (132)

6. The weakening of the parent-child relations is valuable in several ways, according to Frazier. What are they? Are there reasons against this practice? Give your view. (133)

7. Referring to child-rearing, Castle asks, "What happens to 'identification?'" If Walden Two children do not want to be like their parents, how are their personalities developed? What is your response? (134)

8. "The marriage system trades on them!" says Frazier, speaking of the partners' feelings of insecurity. Describe his view of the usual middle-class marriage in America. What is your opinion? (135)

9. "To make matters worse," Frazier complains, "we educate our women as if they were equal, and promise them equality. Is it any wonder they are soon disillusioned?" What does he mean? Have things changed in any significant way since 1948? (136)

10. Frazier claims that some mothers in contemporary society try to make their child more helpless. Why? Do you agree? Would the Walden Two system alleviate this problem? (137)

Values Clarification

Frazier turns his attention to human relations, particularly those between men and women, parents and children. He carefully directs his comments to the young couples, as well as to the professors:

1. On adolescent sex: "Sex is no problem in itself." (121)

2. On teen-age romance: "The glowing adolescent debutante with a string of devoted swains is an artificial bit of trumpery which civilization can well do without." (125)

3. On the family: "The family is an ancient form of community, and the customs and habits which have been set up to perpetuate it are out of place in a society which isn't based on blood ties." (128)

4. On child-rearing: "Home is not the place to rear children." (132)

Think carefully about each of these topics, completely disregarding Frazier's opinions. Place a "B" beside the topic of most importance to teen-age boys, and use a "G" for teen-age girls. The same topic may be marked for both boys and girls.

Consider your results and then prepare a statement on sex differences in values. Are there any rather universal differences? If so, what are they and what are their origins? If not, why not? Reflect on the roles of heredity and environment in these circumstances.

Or prepare a statement on Frazier's views. Do they show a sex bias? Does his approach to the design of Walden Two decrease or increase sex differences? How? Give some attention to the probable future sex differences in values in our own culture.

Part Two
The Talks

". . . we turned and climbed a low ramp to the roof of the
common rooms. Many members were sitting up here in
the early twilight. It was a part of Walden Two of which I
had no hint."

Unit VI
The Good Life
(Chapters 19-22)

What is the good life? The purpose of this unit is to show how it can be defined and how it can be achieved. It also describes the Walden Code and customs, showing how some of the problems in a competitive society might be avoided. In addition, it offers an opportunity to tour the health facilities.

Summary

At dinner, Burris comments on the failure of other attempts at cooperative living, isolated from the rest of the world. "I should think," he adds, "the failure of similar attempts in the past would have some bearing on Walden Two."

Frazier bristles in reply, "Similar! Similar!" he says, almost mockingly. "*How* similar? *How* similar?"

He argues that we only know what their buildings looked like and what the members wrote about, if they were literate. He says he has great respect for these people, and the relevancy of their written works but argues that they tell us little about the psychological management of their communities. "The cultural pattern was usually a matter of revealed truth and not open to experimental modification—except when conspicuously unsuccessful. The community wasn't set up as a real experiment..."

The general approach in these earlier communities, Frazier asserts, was to escape all governmental controls, insofar as possible, thereby allowing natural human virtues to become manifest. "What more can you ask for as an explanation of failure?" he asks. (Chapter 19)

After dinner, the group goes to the roof of the common rooms for a discussion of the good life. When challenged for a definition, Frazier asserts that the good life entails the following conditions: health, minimal unpleasant labor, opportunity to exercise talents and abilities, intimate and satisfying personal contacts, and finally rest and relaxation.

"Is there any doubt that health is better than illness?" he asks, describing his first condition for the good life. Castle points out possible exceptions, when someone might choose ill-health. Frazier resists. "*Other things being equal*," he insists, "we choose health." And there is no further dispute on this point.

"Secondly, can anyone doubt that an absolute minimum of unpleasant labor is part of the Good Life?" Burris replies. "That's the millionaire's idea, anyway."

Frazier points out that he does not want to avoid labor by imposing on others. He simply wants to reduce unpleasant labor to a minimum. "Painful or uninteresting work is a threat to both physical and psychological health." At Walden Two, unpleasant work has been largely eliminated.

"Even hard work is fun if it's not beyond our strength and we don't have too much of it," he adds. "We may even search for work when a scarcity threatens."

The fatal flaw in labor reform, Frazier continues, is that these programs invoke long, dismal campaigns during which the labor leaders attempt to create dissatisfaction and unrest. The reform movement depends in part on increasing the feeling of misery among workers.

"Can you believe," Frazier asks, concluding his argument on a different note, "that most of us have stored up enough spare credits to take a long vacation if we liked?"

"The Good Life also means a chance to exercise talents and abilities," he continues, making his third point. There is time in Walden Two, he says, for arts and crafts, sports and hobbies. But most important is the chance to express interest in the world. This interest, casual or controlled, is an unnecessary exploration of the world, selected and pursued purely for pleasure.

On the fourth point, there is again no debate. "And we need intimate and satisfying personal contacts," Frazier declares. The Social Manager in Walden Two seeks this goal, using various means, discouraging domination and criticism of others, encouraging general tolerance and affection.

"Last of all, the Good Life means rest and relaxation," says Frazier, adding that this condition occurs regularly in Walden Two. The reason is not merely a reduction in labor but also the satisfaction of needs. The leisure class in contemporary society, he points out, may be the least relaxed, struggling "to have a good time" or "to get what they want." True leisure, at Walden Two, is more than a reduced work load.

This approach to the good life, Frazier argues, is not theory but fact. The success of Walden Two gives more than a rational argument; it provides experimental justification.

"How do you keep these conditions in force?" asks Burris.

Frazier replies that happiness cannot be enforced. The key issue is not force. "All we need," he insists, "is adequate behavioral engineering."

Castle asks how these conditions can be put into effect, and Frazier answers that the key lies in certain rules of conduct, the Walden Code. This code is a memory aid until good behavior becomes habitual. Whereupon Frazier proceeds to give some examples of rules of conduct at Walden Two: Do not discuss the operation of the community with outsiders. Give a full explanation of your work to any interested community member. Do not gossip. Express boredom readily.

Since Burris asks specifically for examples of trivial rules, Frazier expounds on the gossip rule. "It was hard to put into effect," he points out. "A valuable rule, of course, in easing personal difficulties."

The Code, he emphasizes, even concerns the social graces. At Walden Two, strangers do not wait to be introduced and do not bother with perfunctory introductions, when there is no clear purpose. The average American may find this custom awkward, but it would cause no embarrassment among the English.

Frazier points to the open expression of boredom, further illustrating the Code for social behavior. It was also a difficult rule to put into practice. But once adopted, the members of Walden Two found it efficient and gratifying, saving many dull moments. They spare themselves by saying: "You've told me that before" or "That's something which I don't find very interesting." Burris decides that the speaker would feel affronted. "Not when the practice is fully accepted," Frazier replies. "It's just a matter of getting used to it."

Castle voices skepticism. Life at Walden Two would not challenge him. Long-term plans are not possible.

Frazier makes a distinction. A few highly intelligent people need distant and magnificent goals, but most people simply do not want to plan that way. Castle asserts that only the latter would be happy in a community like Walden Two, and Frazier argues that such people are the basis of a community—solid and trustworthy.

Then Frazier doubts that highly intelligent people with long-range plans would be unhappy at Walden Two. He asks Castle to send a highly intelligent friend with distant goals to Walden Two, and then, through experimentation, they could decide whether Walden Two is a place for a person with long-range plans. Castle has no specific person in mind. "What about the boy who wants to make a name for himself in some business?" he asks.

Frazier explains that both fame and fortune usually are achieved at others' expense. At Walden Two there is no direct competition and therefore little admiration of others' exceptional achievements. The Code even prohibits the direct expression of thanks. Frazier explains that the community overflows with gratitude, but not to anyone in particular. The people at Walden Two are grateful to all and to none.

If a competent person is not praised, an incompetent person is not blamed. The incompetent individual is simply given other work. Castle asks, "What if a man did poor work, or none at all, in every job you put him on?" Frazier replies that the man would be sent to a psychologist, but it is likely that he would visit the psychologist on his own long before the condition was judged serious.

Frazier, noting Castle's antiexperimental attitude, discusses the value of the experimental approach. "Experimentation with life—could anything be more fascinating?"

"But do you really experiment at all?" Burris asks.

"You mean the 'control,'" says Frazier. "We're too small to keep two groups of children separate," he continues, giving an example. "Some day it may be possible—we shall have controls to satisfy the most academic statistician. And by that time they may be necessary, too, for we shall have reached the point of dealing with very subtle differences. At present they aren't necessary. To go to all the trouble of running controls would be to make a fetish of the scientific method."

To illustrate, Frazier describes a man who complains of fallen arches, dandruff, and eyestrain. Later, when he is completely cured, the physician has no doubt about what led to what. The eyeglasses did not cure the fallen arches or the dandruff; the arch supports had no bearing on the relief from the other problems.

Burris objects. The example is contrived. But then he recalls that in the early stages of any science rapid advances are possible without elaborate statistical controls.

"The happiness and equanimity of our people," Frazier insists, "are *obviously* related to the self-control they have acquired."

Frazier comments on the advantages of a good night's sleep and he heads towards his room. Castle, too, takes his leave of the group. (Chapter 20)

Burris, however, goes for a walk and smokes a cigarette, disconcerted at the lack of enjoyment smoking gives him. He wonders at his recently diminishing consumption of tobacco.

He hears footsteps and realizes that Steve and Mary are looking for him. They ask what he thinks of Walden Two and whether or not Frazier is telling the truth. It then becomes clear that the couple is hopeful about joining Walden Two. When Burris says there should be no question about whether they can join, the couple is elated.

Burris goes to his room, feeling strangely in conflict. He envies Frazier, has grown especially fond of Mary, and wonders about himself for even thinking about living in Walden Two. (Chapter 21)

In the morning, the news that Mary and Steve are joining Walden Two has diverse effects. Burris and Rodge extend their wholehearted congratulations. Barbara and Castle show disapproval. Steve and Mary are happy with their choice, as is Frazier. As usual, Burris continues in his role as mediator.

After the touring party finishes earning labor credits, they go to the medical building. Steve and Mary will take the medical examination, their last requirement for becoming members of Walden Two, and Frazier takes this opportunity to discuss preventive medicine and dentistry. (Chapter 22)

Key Concepts

Write a definition for each of these terms. When in doubt, reread the indicated pages in *Walden Two* and consult the glossary in this guidebook.

the Good Life, 146

the Walden Code, 150

experimental point of view, 162

controls, 163

preventive medicine, 176

preventive dentistry, 177

Illustrations

The concepts in *Walden Two* are often illustrated in daily life. Below are students' illustrations of three concepts in this unit. Supply additional examples yourself of these or other key concepts in this unit.

❦

The Good Life (146). "I just recently discovered the essentials of the 'good life,' and their importance in quality daily existence. This wasn't something to which I had devoted any intellectual or philosophical exercise. No, quite the opposite. I was hit in the face with the fact that my bleeding stomach ulcer was due, at least in part, to a lack of the optimal conditions for human living: a minimum of unpleasant labor, opportunities to use talents and abilities, satisfying personal relationships, adequate rest and relaxation, and good health.

"Now I have not lived a wretched life, totally void of such conditions, but there were a few things that my doctor, and some well-intentioned friends, suggested I change. I was working at a highly stressful, underpaid job where I was also dealing with a certain amount of sexual harassment. The long hours of this job prevented me from taking the courses I so desperately needed to complete my bachelor's degree, hindering my freedom to fully realize my abilities and talents. Third, due to my long hours, coupled with my responsibilities for my children, rest and relaxation were two states I could only imagine, much less enjoy. Of course, I had very little time to spend with my friends, so put another strike next to satisfying relationships. All totaled, these situations contributed to the stress and tension which caused my stomach ulcer: thus the last optimal condition, good health, was no longer something I enjoyed.

"It was very clear that changes were needed. I quit my job, which was the root cause of many other problems. Immediately the tension was lifted, and I had time to pursue my education fully. I was also able to enjoy my children, despite the work of child-rearing, and to spend time with friends occasionally, thus reintroducing quality relationships into my life. Perhaps most importantly, I altered my attitude; no longer did I feel guilty about taking some time everyday just to relax, be it meditation or a long hot bath. These factors have facilitated a speedy recovery, and I am no longer suffering from the painful symptoms of the ulcer."

❦

The Walden Code (150). "As an undergraduate I went to a small private college that had, along with its ethical standards, an honor code. The basis of the Code was that the college was a community, with each member responsible for his or her own conduct and for collectively upholding the standards and ideals of the community. The Code spanned both the academic and social spheres of the college.

"During my senior year I went to a campus discussion about the effectiveness of the Code in the community. Two students expressed concern that while the academic portion of the Code was clear, the social aspect seemed too vague. They felt they needed a set of more specific written rules to follow, almost as if they wanted a checklist of 'honorable' and 'dishonorable' actions. I was disturbed by the lack of understanding of the Code these remarks implied. I asked these students how long they had been at the college. My suspicions were correct! They were freshmen. I went from disturbed to delighted, having answered for myself the question of whether or not the Code was effective. It was by seeing someone else's naivete about the Code that I was able to see my own growth in the years I had been there.

"For me as a senior, the Honor Code needed no more specificity, but more importantly, I realized I no longer abided by the Honor Code because of the college. Instead I liked living my life this way. It was then that I realized I had taken the Honor Code into my life outside of the college."

Preventive medicine (176). "I belong to a clinic which actively concerns itself with preventive medicine. Members receive a newsletter regularly to help them keep up to date on health-related issues. Articles include information on diet and exercise as well as tips for avoiding serious health problems.

"Seminars are also held periodically on a wide range of topics. Through these seminars, members are encouraged to quite smoking, eat a nutritious diet, and follow a regular exercise program. There are also programs which teach people how to deal with stress and cope with family problems. In general, the emphasis in on prevention rather than cure.

"Putting the emphasis on prevention benefits both the clinic and its members. For the clinic, prevention makes sense economically. A seminar on the dangers of cholesterol and fat is cheaper than a bypass operation. For members, there is even more to gain than lower health care costs. Life is a lot more enjoyable when you're physically fit and it lasts longer too."

Study Questions

1. How does Frazier explain the failure of prior utopian communities? What were the usual procedures or guidelines for setting up these communities? What is the basic principle behind the founding of Walden Two? (145)

2. According to Frazier, what are the basic conditions of the Good Life? Give an example of each. (146-149)

3. Give examples of two rules in the Walden Code. Could people in our society abide by these rules? If not, what might be done to make them more effective? (150-151)

4. Explain the Walden Two position on "Thank you." What is your view? (157-158)

5. What is done with violators of the Walden Code? How does this approach compare with your conception of the use of punishment? (159)

6. Burris and Frazier have quite different views about the need for control in experimental studies. Explain each position. (163)

7. When may members of Walden Two be asked to undergo physical examinations? What is your reaction to this practice? Does it seem worth the cost? (176)

8. Who, if anyone, controls the diet of members of the Walden Two community? What is your view of this procedure? (176)

9. What are the regulations for medical patients in Walden Two with regard to exercise, sunshine, fresh air, and rest? Does this approach seem appropriate to you? Why or why not? (176)

10. What is it like to be a dentist in Walden Two? Why? To which type of dentistry is most time devoted? Why? (177)

Values Clarification

The tour is complete, except for the medical center, and the extensive talks begin. Frazier states his five conditions for the Good Life and adds:

1. On work: "Even hard work is fun if it's not beyond our strength and we don't have too much of it." (147)

2. On personal favors: "Things run more smoothly if we don't hand out tokens of gratitude and if we conceal personal contributions." (157)

3. On experimenting in daily life: "To go to all the trouble of running controls would be to make a fetish of the scientific method." (163)

4. On rest: "The simple fact is our civilization puts no value on rest." (165)

Imagine that you have become a Manager in Walden Two. A group responsible for founding Walden Three asks you to become Manager of Public Relations in that new community. One of your tasks is to convince potential converts to Walden Three of the importance of the customs and Code in Walden Two.

Using the indicated page numbers, reread the relevant passages. Afterward, ignoring Frazier's remarks, indicate the order of these topics, 1st through 4th, according to their importance in your orientation program for prospective new members. Remember that you are trying to help them understand Walden Two.

Think carefully about the most important topic. Then develop a brief statement explaining the Walden Two position on that topic and why it is so important, referring to Frazier's comment if you wish. The basic aim is to show how Walden Two and contemporary society regard this topic differently and how this difference can be vital in the success of Walden Three.

"'By no means. I'm not arguing for no government at all,
but only for none of the existing forms. We want a
government based upon a science of human behavior.'"

Unit VII
Politics and Propaganda
(Chapters 23-26)

Government, religion, and other social institutions are considered in this unit. Its purpose is to show the value of experimentation, rather than indoctrination. Coercing obedience or gaining it through propaganda, Frazier asserts, ensures failure. Experiments are the only way to answer questions about human nature and the optimal conditions for human life.

Summary

As the visitors enter the serving room for lunch, Frazier says that there is not much left to show them. He wonders whether they have been impressed.

"'Impressed' is scarcely the word," says Burris. "It's the most soul-shaking experience of my life."

But Frazier claims the success of Walden Two is not at all incredible. "How could it possibly have failed?" he asks. What impresses him is the fact that Walden Two is already in existence, here and now, in the middle of modern civilization.

"The Utopias *have* tended to be a bit out of things," Castle observes.

Excitedly, Frazier agrees and elaborates on the point. "Utopia" in Greek means "nowhere," which Butler spelled almost backwards for his utopian novel, *Erewhon*. Other utopian writers—Bacon, Bellamy, and Morris—imagined their communities in far-away places: undiscovered islands, lost colonies, centuries earlier, or at some unforeseen point in the future.

"Out of things, indeed!" he concludes. "It's the first rule of the Utopian romance: 'Get away from life as we know it, either in space or time, or no one will believe you!'"

"The Good Life is waiting for us—here and now," he declares, emphasizing that the necessary techniques are available, both material and psychological, to develop full and satisfying lives for all humanity.

Castle claims that he still must solve the practical problems of politics, and a conversation ensues about government, power, and human nature. Governments based on force, Frazier claims, are using poor principles of human engineering. The problem with governments is that they cannot—or do not—experiment, chiefly because they cannot admit doubt or ignorance. An ideal government, says Frazier, would be based upon the science of human behavior. Anarchy would not be successful because there is no such thing as innate goodness.

Frazier clarifies his position. "I'm not arguing for no government at all, but only for none of the existing forms....For the first time in history we're ready for it, because we can now deal with human behavior in accordance with simple scientific principles."

"We have no truck with philosophies of innate goodness—or evil, either, for that matter," Frazier continues, describing the Walden Two outlook. "But we do have faith in our power to change human behavior." We can *make* ourselves adequate for group living, he insists. Originally he simply had faith in that premise, but he declares it's now a fact.

Then he proceeds to explain Walden Two's political position in relation to the rest of society. All members vote in state and local elections, but they do not take an interest in outside politics. Instead, the Political Manager researches the qualifications of the candidates in these elections and draws up the "Walden Ticket," whereupon everyone goes to the polls and votes for the candidates who would best serve Walden Two, as identified by the Political Manager. Thus, the members choose the best candidates for their purposes, yet they save time by having the Political Manager inform them about this complex matter.

The conversation turns to another institution, religion. Walden Two, explains Frazier, is not a religious community because the conception of humanity does not come from theology but rather from scientific study. There is no formal religious training although some practices of organized religion are used to inspire group loyalty and to strengthen observance of the Code. Such practices include Sunday meetings with some type of music and occasional readings—philosophical, religious, or poetic. These readings often prompt literary allusions in the speech of the community. The topics chosen for discussion usually concern self-control and social relations.

"But are you taking any active step toward world peace?" Castle asks.

"Any active step!" Frazier cries. "Just this: we aren't making war! We have no imperialist policy—no designs on the possessions of others—no interest in foreign trade except to encourage happiness and self-sufficiency."

No international expert, Frazier argues, really *knows* for certain what sort of society or government will produce peace. These experts only make guesses, with no significant experimental tests. (Chapter 23)

As the group leaves the dining room Burris asks how the community deals with young people drawn away from Walden Two by the modernized world: the movie palaces, nightclubs and fancy restaurants.

"By indoctrination, I suppose," he says.

Frazier objects, replying that the community does not propagandize in favor of its way of life. Instead, the members simply tell the children the whole truth. They make sure that, along with the glamour, the children observe the saloons, the jails, and the homes for the indigents. They help the children understand that the glamour and beautiful homes and landscapes are available only to a few and often at the expense of poverty and filth for many.

Burris asks again why indoctrination is not used at Walden Two, and Frazier replies that it would ensure failure. It is impossible, he says, to propagandize and experiment simultaneously. Therefore, Walden Two operates without propaganda. To indoctrinate favorable attitudes toward Walden Two, he continues, would conceal symptoms of unrest which would be studied by the community psychologists. Walden Two should be naturally satisfying. Happiness therefore is one of the measures of success of the community.

As this discussion draws to a close, Steve and Mary appear. They have passed the medical exam and been accepted into the Walden Two community. (Chapter 24)

Burris, impressed with the pleasant atmosphere in Walden Two, decides to make his own investigation of happiness. To make sure the guests are not being deceived, he mingles with the members at tea time to take a sample of their behavior.

He lays out a plan which clearly illustrates his loyalty to scientific procedures, using an objective sampling procedure. He begins at the bottom of the Ladder at four o'clock and progresses to each successive stage, eavesdropping on the occupants of each alcove for exactly five minutes.

This survey of conversations in the Ladder leaves him dissatisfied. He stops in several different areas, then goes to the lounges and reading rooms, still without finding signs of psychological problems. Wandering aimlessly, he slips into a music room to listen to a string quartet accompanied by a pianist who is out of his line of vision. The string players are young, competent, and poised; the pianist seems a little less capable. At the conclusion of the piece, Burris discovers that the pianist is Frazier. (Chapter 25)

Walking back to his room, Burris believes that his survey has failed, and then he realizes that there was a flaw in his objectivity. He was not out to collect facts but rather to find something wrong with Walden Two. He feels he is caught in a difficult position, not ready to join Walden Two but unable to find anything clearly wrong with it.

He also decides that his survey was conducted improperly. He had made it at a time when people should be happy. Instead, he needs a longitudinal study. He should follow one member around for an extended period.

Just as he makes this decision, he notices an apparently typical woman sitting outside alone. Mrs. Olsen initiates the conversation, and Burris eagerly tries to gather information. He finds she is puzzled by his questions, appearing happy, healthy, and well fed. He is also impressed that she can be content with so little to do. As he heads for his room, Burris is clearly frustrated, not so much with Walden Two as with his own cynicism that only hard labor could prevent boredom. (Chapter 26)

Key Concepts

Write a definition for each of these terms. When in doubt, reread the indicated pages in *Walden Two* and consult the glossary in this guidebook.

human engineering, 181

human nature, 182

indoctrination, 191

propaganda, 194

objective sampling, 197

longitudinal study, 203

Illustrations

The concepts in *Walden Two* are often illustrated in daily life. Below are students' illustrations of three concepts in this unit. Supply additional examples yourself of these or other key concepts in this unit.

Human engineering (181). "A few years ago a mall was built in my hometown. It was seen as a new concept in shopping for that area and became extremely popular very quickly. Its shape is somewhat like that of a snake with smooth curves and no sharp corners. Thus, it seems small and cozy, without long halls. The shops themselves vary greatly in both size and content. One can find small specialty boutiques and right around the corner a major department store. And, uncommon to most stores, the Mall extends its hours and is open seven days a week. During the holidays, decorations add a 'home-like' atmosphere, and continual shows and displays make the mall more than a place to shop. With these benefits, people actually enjoy the Mall as a place to visit, relax, and meet friends, as well."

Human nature (182). "What is your view of human nature? Are we innately good or innately evil? My answer is: 'Neither.' Our personalities are largely what the environment makes us.

"No one can run an experiment of this sort, but I think the difference between my ethnic, hometown friends and my school friends says something. Their two environments seem to produce somewhat different types of people, with different habits and interests.

"My home-town friends love their environment with no exams, no special deadlines. At the end of the workday, we begin an evening of fun and relaxation, in a sort of ethnic style, and the most essential part is being with friends. The atmosphere is relaxed, and we get together simply to be with each other, to talk and think together, discussing the humor—and problems—of the day. There is an implicit acceptance of the idea that to be with friends is the most significant part of life, certainly more important than individual accomplishments.

"Here at school the environment is almost the opposite. We get together for fun, but the atmosphere is chiefly competitive, or at least the work ethic prevails. We study for exams, read books at great length, write papers, compete on teams, compete for positions on school activities and the like, often until midnight or afterward. Evenings are devoted to 'getting ahead.' The motivation is for personal achievement, more than for friends. The focus in on the individual, more than the group.

"Exceptions exist, of course. My ethnic friends have certain personal goals and my school friends cherish certain personal relations. But there is a large, overall difference between these groups, and the environment seems chiefly responsible. Neither approach is obviously better or worse than the other, but when this idea is extended to the different influences of street gangs and loving families, I find the notion of an inborn human nature very dubious indeed."

Indoctrination (191). "I grew up in an extremely religious environment.

"We children were not allowed to see any movies that the elders didn't approve of, and we could not play cards, have friends outside the religion, or go into town alone. I went to the service on Sundays, church school on Tuesdays, had home studies on Wednesdays, meeting again on Thursdays, and field service activities on Saturdays. I was taught that the world would probably end before I turned 12 years old. I was told that if I had sexual relations with someone before getting married, no one would want me and I couldn't enter into heaven. We never celebrated any holidays except one and were told that this shouldn't bother us because people should not worship pagan things.

"The women were discouraged from being feminine and from wearing pants. They were taught to be submissive and passive instead. The men were taught to be leaders and headstrong. The members of this community do not vote, smoke, curse, or consider themselves a part of this world except as teachers of the unfortunate many who are misled by the devil.

"Due to this indoctrination, they believe the world is basically an evil place, largely to be avoided. When some members do leave the community, out of protest or for some other reason, they often have considerable difficulty. Without a balanced perspective, and especially without developing critical thinking, they cannot adjust readily to other ways of life."

Study Questions

1. "You can't make progress toward the Good Life by political action! Not under *any* current form of government!" says Frazier. What are his reasons for this statement? In your answer, define what he means by government and politics. (180)

2. Frazier says government should be based on the science of human behavior rather than faith in human nature. Define these two expressions, as he uses them, and indicate the reasons for his position. State your position. (182)

3. Describe the work of the Political Manager in Walden Two. How does this role differ from that of political campaign managers in our contemporary society? (183)

4. What is the chief responsibility of the Manager of Public Relations? How does he or she carry out these responsibilities? What is Frazier's view of this behavior? Your view? (184-186)

5. Describe the ways in which religious practices in Walden Two are like those in the outside world. Describe the differences. Be specific. (185)

6. Castle asks Frazier how the community would wage war in the case of attack. What is Frazier's response? What is your view of his response? (189)

7. Engage in a Walden Two detective assignment, showing in the briefest way a connection between a bit of luxury and some instance of poverty. Do so beginning with a luxurious hotel suite. What arguments can you make on behalf of these circumstances? (192)

8. "You can't propagandize and experiment at the same time," says Frazier. Explain his view. Do you agree or disagree? Why? (195)

9. Burris decides to sample happiness in Walden Two, stopping at several different stages or alcoves in the Ladder to observe and ask questions. Does this procedure seem to be an objective, unbiased approach? If so, why? If not, why not? (197-202)

10. Describe Burris' encounter with Mrs. Olsen. What does she think of him? What is his reaction to her? What is your reaction to this scene? (204)

Values Clarification

"We've shot our bolt," says Frazier when the group returns from the medical center. "I'm curious to know whether you've been properly impressed."

Castle calls the tour a soul-shaking experience. But he declares that the problem of government and politics has not been resolved. Frazier has commented extensively on this issue:

1. On using power in government: "Governments which use force are based upon bad principles of human engineering." (181)

2. On innate goodness: "We have no truck with philosophies of innate goodness—or evil, either, for that matter." (182)

3. On voting: "No one of us believes his weight will be felt in a national election." (188)

4. On the dangers of indoctrination: "You can't propagandize and experiment at the same time." (195)

These topics all pertain to government. Focusing upon Frazier's remarks, indicate the topic which you think he considers most important by writing "FRAZIER" in front of that statement. Then imagine the choice of the President of the United States or prime minister of some other country. Write "POLITICIAN" in front of that topic, which may or may not be the same as your choice for Frazier.

Prepare a presentation, oral or written, on the ways in which these choices reflect similar or different values. What other values probably accompany each choice? What factors influence these values? Include an explanation of your own viewpoint.

Review

Castle is resistant to the concept of Walden Two, yet the tours and talks have been unsettling for him. Reconsider units I through V and for each unit indicate one or two basic values Castle displays. Then note which of these seem to have been challenged by his experience in the community.

I. Breaking Away

II. Design of Things

III. Working, Playing

IV. Raising Children

V. Marriage and the Family

A person's values usually are consistent with one another. Try to show how there is a consistency or congruence among the values you have cited for Augustine Castle.

"The top of the desk was littered. . . . Books were piled irregularly on the floor . . . and one pile was topped with a bundle of soiled clothes. Half a dozen canvases on stretchers were stacked. . . ."

Unit VIII
Beyond Heroes
(Chapters 27-28)

Walden Two is a place without heroes. This unit demonstrates that personal figures, such as leaders and heroes, supplement a faulty science of human behavior. It provides an opportunity for discussion of fascism, democracy, and the place of history in education. Frazier feels that history is often in error and unnecessarily promotes heroes.

Summary

During an early evening stroll, Frazier, Castle, and Burris observe the arrival of four or five trucks containing many people, young and old, the advance guard of Walden Six, a community seventy miles away. They are met by an enthusiastic group of about one hundred members of Walden Two. Walden Six is not yet a full-fledged community, and most of its members are former members of Walden Two. Frazier explains that Waldens Three, Four, and Five are fashioned after his Walden, but they have no direct relationship with Walden Two. Only Walden Six involved a transfer of membership. The name of Walden Two, he points out, was chosen from Thoreau's Walden, an experiment in living. But it involved only one person and ignored many social questions.

A conversation ensues about the assimilation of new members. Burris wonders what would happen if a large crowd wanted to join Walden Two. Frazier replies that Burris has asked an experimental question and explains that at this point Walden Two is not taking any risks. There will be no large-scale additions yet.

Burris wonders whether an undesirable new member is capable of corrupting the Walden Two children or causing trouble in the community. Frazier laughs, assuring Burris that the members of Walden Two would not be disrupted. In fact, the community gradually would supply a countereducation for the new member.

Frazier continues with the idea of expansion, pointing out that if labor credit requirements were increased, growth would be much faster. In thirty years, he explains, Walden Two could easily absorb the entire country. But by requiring more work, the community would sacrifice one of its most important principles.

Rapid growth would bring many other problems. The assimilation of large numbers of converts would not be possible, and these people would find it difficult to proceed without benefit of the Walden Two scientific practices. Furthermore, the transmission of the necessary technical information for all departments would be prohibitive.

The Office of Information, he explains, was established to control publicity, not to create it. A glowing account would lead to the frightening prospect of large-scale expansion. The community will be ready for it, he adds, in five or ten years.

As Frazier divulges his long-range plans for a Walden Two civilization, Castle becomes increasingly restless. No monopolist, he cries, ever was more ruthless. He accuses Frazier of fascism, of creating a dictatorship.

"But who's the dictator here?"

"Why, you, of course," replies Castle.

Frazier admits to being the prime mover, but now there is no need to push his ideas. That's the whole point, he exclaims. If the community is properly established, through experimentation, it will operate by itself.

Burris comes to his defense, remembering his encounter with Mrs. Olsen. "As a matter of fact," he says, "I ran into a woman this afternoon who had some difficulty in placing you when I mentioned your name."

Frazier smiles. Burris becomes suspicious. Had Mrs. Olsen been placed in his path intentionally?

Walden Two has no heroes, Frazier explains. "We have got beyond all that."

A culture which has emerged through experiments, he continues, does not need strong personal leadership. In fact, it should contain several guarantees against it. The members of Walden Two do not act for the benefit of anyone else unless they are serving as agents of the community. The cultural engineers have destroyed personal favoritism, just as they have eliminated personal gratitude. No individual is in debt to anyone or any group, except to the whole community.

The planning and managerial procedures of Walden Two are deliberately concealed. Apart from the Managers, Frazier speculates, only a half-dozen people could identify correctly all six Planners.

A sense of history is discouraged for this same reason. There is no public celebration of the founding of Walden Two, no recognition of seniority, no special regard for early members. The Legal Manager maintains a log of the community's history, useful only to Planners and Managers.

Some historic figures have been despotic, Castle acknowledges, but certainly not all of them. Many have been benevolent. Frazier agrees but adds that even benevolent leaders have a place only when government is an art. The leader is useful only when the science is defective. The Planners of Walden Two act successfully in almost complete anonymity.

Walden Two, Frazier proclaims, does not need personal figures, either as specialists or as a means of holding power. "A society which functions for the good of all cannot tolerate the emergence of individual figures... A society without heroes has almost fabulous strength."

Skill and strength, for example, are valued at Walden Two but not for personal triumph, as in a competitive society. The heroes, if they can be called that, are not people who defeat others but rather those who triumph over themselves or over nature. They are people who dive with grace or vault over a high bar, on a par with musicians, dressmakers, or cattle breeders.

In Walden Two, therefore, the members are not taught history, which usually promotes heroes. Those who enjoy it may read all they wish, but it is not considered essential in their education.

Castle says that history gives a perspective, but Frazier counters that it is also oversimplified. Any historical event is too complex to be known by anyone. Nothing is more confusing to an evaluation of the present, he says, than a sense of history. The issue is the *now*. And it is the only condition which can be studied scientifically. (Chapter 27)

As they prepare for Sunday breakfast, Burris is still wondering whether Frazier is a fascist. Castle resolves to ask him about the dignity and integrity of the individual.

At breakfast, Frazier seats himself next to Barbara, apparently to encourage her, and Rodge as well, to join the community. However, it is obvious that Barbara has other thoughts entirely, and Frazier appears foolish.

The group prepares to attend Sunday service, and as they start toward the theater, Frazier invites Burris to forgo the event. It appears that he wants to talk privately with Burris.

Frazier asks Burris about the relationship between Rodge and Barbara. Clearly, the young man wants to join Walden Two, but Barbara would never consent. Frazier resolves that he will have a word with Rodge.

When they enter Frazier's personal room, Burris is struck by the disorder. Everything is in chaos. Frazier points out that his room is his castle, the precision in his thinking is matched only by the disorder in his personal habits.

Frazier immediately broaches the subject which seems to be bothering him. He claims that Burris' attitude toward Walden Two is really an attitude toward him. "Quite frankly, Burris, why do you dislike me?" Then he adds: "You think I'm conceited, aggressive, tactless, selfish... Of all the people you've seen in the past four days, you're sure that I'm *one*, at least, who couldn't possibly be a genuine member of any community."

Eventually, in his own defense, Frazier explains that he is not a product of Walden Two. The final social structure toward which he is working must await those with a full Walden Two heritage. He is one of the pots that were marred in the making. (Chapter 28)

Key Concepts

Write a definition for each of these terms. When in doubt, reread the indicated pages in *Walden Two* and consult the glossary in this guidebook.

Walden Six, 208

Walden, 209

competitive society, 216

democracy, 217

fascism, 219

personal figures, 221

Illustrations

The concepts in *Walden Two* are often illustrated in daily life. Below are students' illustrations of three concepts in this unit. Supply additional examples yourself of these or other key concepts in this unit.

❧❧❧

Walden Six (208). "I don't know about Walden Six, which of course is fictional too, but I once went to a community in northern Mexico like Walden Two and perhaps Six, as well. In operation for 15 years, Los Horcones was founded with the purpose of applying the basic principle of Walden Two in a rural setting.

"Jamie, one of the 30 or so members, gave me a complete tour, including the community living and dining rooms, some of the members' private rooms, the children's house, workshops, school, orchards, gardens, animals' pastures and other areas. Then I decided to stay a while as a guest. As in Walden Two, I paid for my stay by earning labor credits, usually by assisting the teachers with normal and retarded learners. I chose this assignment from a list of community tasks prepared by the work managers.

"The children in Los Horcones all live together in their own house. A special staff is in charge of their welfare, and a list of behavioral objectives has been developed in order to achieve these goals. The principles of reinforcement are carefully applied but there are no grades. Instead, there are flexible study schedules and each child keeps track of his or her progress on a personal chart.

"Also like Walden Two, there is a behavior code, chiefly concerned with cooperation, pacifism, and equality, but it can be adjusted as new needs arise. And there is an orientation toward preventive medicine, emphasizing adequate physical activity and a balanced diet of natural foods. Smoking is permitted only by those in the process of giving up the habit.

"They send out a regular announcement about their activities. It's called the 'Walhdos Newsletter.'

"If interested, you can write to arrange a visit: Comunidad Los Horcones, Apdo. 372, Hermosillo, Sonora 83000, Mexico. I hope you enjoy your stay, as I certainly did."

❧❧❧

Competitive society (216). "Once I managed a restaurant for __ Ice Cream. This position offered me a unique opportunity to 'manage' the small society of 30 employees.

"In the final weeks of a recent year, it became apparent that the company was to fall several hundred thousand dollars short of its projected sales. In response, headquarters required each division manager to submit a plan for increasing sales 10% over the projection for the last four weeks of the year. Therefore, my division manager, an autocratic, highly competitive man, decreed that each of his 49 restaurants would hold a contest: at the end of the four-week period, the employee in that restaurant with the highest average increase per-customer sale would receive a television set.

"I persuaded him to allow me to pursue a different course. The average per-customer sale would be computed for each employee, but every employee who increased his average by 15% or more over the four-week period would receive a free half gallon of ice cream and a pat on the back. Furthermore, if we as a team exceeded our 10% goal and achieved a 15% increase, the cost of the TV would be doubled and the money would be converted into a party for the entire team.

71

"With our most experienced employees coaching others on sales techniques and everyone pulling together as a team, we realized a 17% increase over projected sales. Only two other restaurants in our district achieved the 10% goal, and none matched our 17%. The reason? In the other restaurants the employees were often trying to get ahead at one another's expense. The aim was simply to beat the next guy. In ours, everyone worked toward the same goal because it was of benefit to all."

Personal figures (221). "The benefits of discouraging any sense of history and eliminating seniority perhaps can be illustrated by my trip last year to Las Vegas with my tennis team to play in the National Amateur Championships. The trip was the culmination of several years of trying to qualify. In getting to Vegas, it was important that we didn't remember and didn't care who won all the necessary matches or who garnered the bonus points that allowed us a bye in the first round. Eight members of the team had worked together for 3 years, and two first-year members assimilated quickly into the team. All of us equally reaped the benefits of previous hard work.

"All players had equal responsibility to go out and try to win for the team. We had no dominant figure, although the team captain kept a historical log of match outcomes. Whether an individual won or lost a match was significant only to the total team score. History of team, length of time on team, past team heroes, etc... had no bearing on what we were doing in that present environment. (Off the courts we had a Gambling Manager to advise as to disposal of extra labor credits!!!)"

Study Questions

1. "That's an experimental question," Frazier replies, when asked about the expansion of Walden Two. What does he mean? Explain how he would proceed. (211)

2. "How do you take in a new member?" Burris asks. "Is there some sort of legal contract?" Describe the agreement between the new member and Walden Two. (213)

3. Explain Frazier's view of democracy. Take into consideration his position in national versus local politics. What are its advantages and disadvantages? (217)

4. "A society without heroes has an almost fabulous strength," says Frazier. What does he mean by this remark? Explain the hero's function in a society not based on a science of human behavior. (222)

5. Give some thought to the President of the United States as a role model for children in Walden Two. To Babe Ruth. How would Frazier feel? Why? (222)

6. Frazier challenges the accuracy of historical facts. But many technological advances since the 1940s should improve the accuracy of history. Would these influence his view that we can make no real use of history? Explain your reasons. (223)

7. "The hero, my dear Mr. Castle, is a device which the historian has taken over from the layman. He uses it because he has no scientific vocabulary or technique for dealing with the facts of history." Explain Frazier's argument about the repetitions of historical events. Do you agree or disagree? Explain your own view. (224)

8. "Your personal relations—are you always so—*scientific*?" Barbara asks, implying that Frazier is more interested in studying people than in enjoying them. How does he reply? Cite his example of the botanist. (228)

9. Note the condition of Frazier's personal room. What does this it suggest about him? About his life in Walden Two? (231)

10. Frazier complains that he is not a product of Walden Two. Why? What is meant by the expression "the pots that were marred in the making"? (234)

Values Clarification

Frazier's one-liners are the hallmark of his style. In this unit, he gives his views on heroes, villains, culture, and history. As usual, he is brash, even brusque:

1. On antisocial behavior: "Society has made the criminal and must take care of him." (212)

2. On prominent people: "The leader or hero supplements a faulty science." (221)

3. On a cooperative culture: "A society which functions for the good of all cannot tolerate the emergence of individual figures." (222)

4. On the uses of history: "Nothing confuses our evaluation of the present more than a sense of history—unless it's a sense of destiny." (224)

Place a plus (+) beside the comment with which you agree most. That viewpoint is high in your list of values, relative to the others.

With which of Frazier's comments do you agree least? Place a minus (-) preceding that remark.

Develop your ideas for a presentation on either comment, plus or minus, making an argument for or against it. Prepare a brief attention-catching introduction; enumerate and support the main points in your argument; and provide a conclusion which reaffirms your position.

Review

Without looking back at units I through V, which describe the tours of Walden Two, indicate the cultural practice or outlook you found most interesting in each unit. If necessary, reexamine the relevant passages. Then cite the principle you feel is most important.

I. Breaking Away

II. Design of Things

III. Working, Playing

IV. Raising Children

V. Marriage and the Family

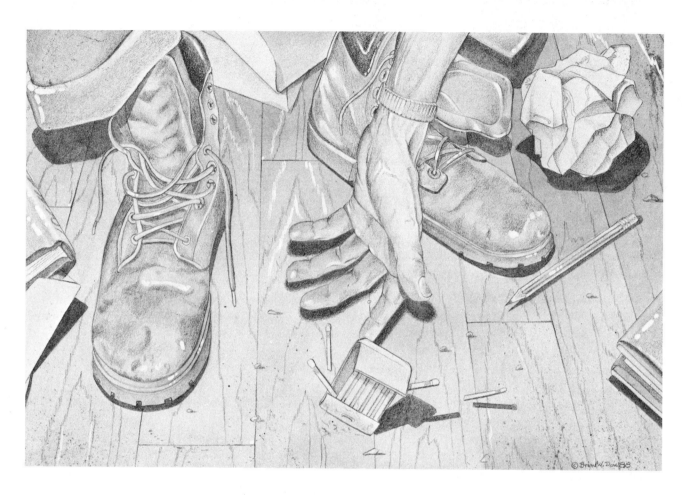

"'You will, of course, do one or the other,' said
Frazier. . . . 'I suggest that as an orderly person you will
probably hold—ah! you drop them! Well, you see, that's
all part of your behavior with respect to me.'"

Unit IX
The Question of Freedom
(Chapters 29-31)

The problem of free will versus determinism is a fundamental issue in Walden Two. The purpose in this unit is to demonstrate that everyone is controlled in one way or another. Through the use of positive reinforcement, rather than punishment, people have the feeling of freedom.

Summary

Since his arrival at Walden Two, Castle has been waiting to discuss the "general issues" mentioned earlier. When the young couples leave for a concert, he and Burris go to Frazier's personal room, where he broaches the subject again, beginning a long debate with Frazier. "I accuse you of one of the most diabolical machinations in the history of mankind!"

Castle explains that the structure of the community is misleading because it appears that Frazier has no power, no current contact with its members. In the beginning, however, he was a despot. He set things up so that eventually he could withdraw himself as a force.

Frazier denies having current power and being a despot. He does admit that he exerted an early influence. Nevertheless, he planned Walden Two as a scientist. "What would you do," he asks, "if you found yourself in possession of an effective science of behavior?"

Castle would dump it in the ocean in favor of giving people their freedom. Frazier answers that Castle then would leave control to the charlatan, the bully, the demagogue, the salesman, and others already knowledgeable about the techniques of behavioral engineering.

As long as there is a trace of personal freedom, Castle declares, he will maintain his position. Frazier, in response, denies that freedom exists at all.

They decide to classify the determiners of human behavior. First, there are physical restraints, such as handcuffs and iron bars. Second, there is the threat of force. At this point Castle says that he sees no other possibilities, but Frazier says there is tremendous power of another sort. He is referring to positive control.

A person's behavior can be controlled, he explains, by creating situations he likes or by taking him out of situations he does not like. He will behave as we want him to if we create positive outcomes, thereby increasing the probability that he will behave that way again. This procedure is called positive reinforcement.

Punishment often appears successful because the behavior is temporarily suppressed, but in the long run it has many undesirable consequences and also is ineffective. The person's *potential* behavior has not been altered—he will still want to repeat the act. The immediate but temporary effect of using punishment, Frazier explains, often overshadows the long-term advantage of positive reinforcement.

Restraint is one form of control, continues Frazier, but absence of restraint is not freedom. There are still compelling forces at work.

People perceive themselves to be free when there is no restraint or no threat of force, but they neglect to examine the positive control of behavior. We never rebel against these forces, he explains, partly because we are not so aware of them, partly because we have no adequate vocabulary for talking about them. It is curious, he concludes, that the question of freedom never arises with positive reinforcement.

He boasts a bit about Walden Two. "By skillful planning, by a wise choice of techniques we *increase* the feeling of freedom."

Castle returns to his concern about power, asserting that Frazier is in complete control, a long-range dictator. Frazier is inclined to agree. Once a person has grasped the principle of positive reinforcement, he can enjoy almost unlimited power. But this power is not despotism; it must be used for the good of others. When it is not, it is reduced by a corresponding amount, says Frazier.

Castle then turns from despotism to democracy, and Frazier counters that democracy is ineffective. No person has a chance of deciding the issue in a national election; the general population is not in a position to evaluate the candidates anyway; and the candidates, when elected, cannot experiment for fear of being voted out of office. They simply maintain the status quo.

What we need, Frazier says, is a government for the benefit of *all*—both the majority *and* the minority. Walden Two, he claims, is closer to the ideal democracy than is democracy in America today, in which election campaigns falsify or obscure the issues. Members of Walden Two do not want an active part in government but merely a guarantee of personal rights, including the opportunity to protest unsatisfactory conditions. No one worries about the operation of the government any more than about the operation of a diesel engine. Both are left to experts.

Castle counters that despots might arise. Frazier agrees that despotic cultures can last for some time, but eventually they are replaced by competing cultures which work more efficiently. The Planners in Walden Two, understanding this principle, avoid the usurpation of power, which would only destroy the community.

They might abscond with funds, Castle retorts. Our only wealth is our happiness, Frazier replies. The physical plant, without its members, is practically worthless.

"But it's human to dominate," says Castle.

"That's an experimental question," Frazier responds.

The Planners, Frazier emphasizes, rule through positive reinforcement. They have no machinery for threat or force. To extend their powers they would need to create more and more satisfying conditions, a curious despotism.

Democracy, he continues, is clearly superior to despotism, as demonstrated in World War II, but it is not the best form of government because it is based on a scientifically invalid concept, the inherent goodness and wisdom of humanity. Democracy ignores the fact that people are made wise and good or foolish and bad by their environments.

Burris points out that people mold the environment and the environment molds people. Which comes first? For Frazier, the question is irrelevant. A beginning has been made; now the problem is to develop the environment in socially useful ways.

Finally, when Burris suggests a resemblance between Russian communism and Walden Two, Frazier states that the Russian plan, as originally conceived, had good potential. But it developed four fundamental weaknesses: (1) a decline in the experimental spirit, which prevents further progress; (2) overpropagandizement of its people and outsiders, suppressing evaluation of its success; (3) the use of heroes, making the process of government an art, rather than a science; and (4) continued use of power, a temporary expedient at the outset but now inappropriate and self-defeating. These conditions leave the Russians far from a culture with a common good. The people do not behave as they want to, says Frazier angrily, spitting into a flowerpot. (Chapter 29)

Burris decides that Castle is right, that Frazier prefers to avoid general issues, founding Walden Two on specific behavioral techniques. Burris agrees, furthermore, that the issue of freedom might never arise in Walden Two and that Castle's concern about despotism might be simply a practical problem in defining the roles of the Managers.

The animated discussion had not added to the visitors' understanding of Walden Two, however. With Frazier leading the way, the trio proceeds to the common rooms, where they observe people enjoying themselves. As Frazier leaves his guests, he makes a date for dining with them at seven. (Chapter 30)

After the simple Sunday night supper, Burris and Castle take a stroll. Castle thinks he won the debate, Burris decides, and Frazier probably thinks the same of himself. The philosopher and behavioral scientist never met on the same field.

The pair return to their room, where Castle begins grading term papers and a thoughtful Burris lies on his bunk. He is in a turmoil about Walden Two. (Chapter 31)

Key Concepts

Write a definition for each of these terms. When in doubt, reread the indicated pages in *Walden Two* and consult the glossary in this guidebook.

despotism, 238

freedom, 240

positive reinforcement, 244

punishment, 244

reinforcement theory, 244

cooperative society, 245

Illustrations

The concepts in *Walden Two* are often illustrated in daily life. Below are students' illustrations of three concepts in this unit. Supply additional examples yourself of these or other key concepts in this unit.

❧❦❧

Freedom (240). "In high school I had a teacher whose methods were drastically different from those used by the rest of the faculty. It was the same school, same students, and the objectives of this teacher and the rest of the faculty were the same—to create the best possible learning environment.

"In the other classes, we never felt free to make the decision to attend class or complete the homework assignments. It felt like we were under the rule of dictators. Failure to adhere to the rules resulted in detention or loss of privileges. To obtain a good grade we had to be obedient. We did not feel free and behaved in ways that interfered with our learning process and at times disrupted the class.

"This one teacher didn't enforce all of the school policies. If a class was missed he did not care if it was unexcused or if the student had a legitimate excuse. His policy was if more than three classes were missed, five points were deducted from the final grade. This gave us a sense of freedom. We could decide whether or not to attend class without the threat of the usual disciplinary measures. However, he prepared the class so we benefitted by choosing to attend. For example there were usually two quizzes each week; if the reading assignment was done each quiz was so easy it was almost a gift, an automatic A. He also structured the writing assignments so they were easier if we had participated in class discussion.

"Although we felt free to attend or not attend class and to do or not do the homework assignment, the teacher carefully designed the class so we chose to do both. The only difference between the typical class and his was the environment. One robbed us of the feeling of freedom and the other, although we were controlled, gave a sense of freedom and encouraged us to do what the teacher wanted us to do—learn."

❧❦❧

Reinforcement theory (244). "Two years ago, as a counselor at an all-boys camp, I was in charge of eight boys, all about ten years old. The kids were pretty well behaved—with the exception of one boy named Sam. He was an overweight, uncoordinated child who was very insecure in the presence of his peers. He alleviated his insecurity by talking back to me and by using bad language, thereby demonstrating to his peers how 'mature' he was.

"It was a very difficult task deciding how I should attempt to change his behavior. I tried a few methods which proved unsuccessful, but then I realized that Sam's rudeness only resulted from his desire for the attention of his peers, and so I decided to approach the problem using this as reinforcement.

"I asked for the cooperation of the other members of the cabin and this was how I set it up: Whenever Sam talked back to me, his peers were to give him the 'silent treatment,' ignoring him. Sam at first did not change his ways. Rather, he increased his obnoxious fits. However, after a couple of days, he became less prone to rudeness. At the same time, I was careful to be extra nice whenever he behaved more normally to me. I quickly encouraged him at all opportunities, which were rare at first.

"With this 'punishment' from his peers and my support for politeness, eventually he became a fairly agreeable kid. The change was really unbelievable."

Punishment (244). "When I was a pre-teen I had an insatiable urge to swipe stuff from shopkeepers in my neighborhood. I would go out at dusk with my usual companion and knock off three or four places in the course of an hour. Over the summer duping the store owners as well as my parents led to a more cocky and relaxed style of this illegal act. Ultimately I got caught one night by my father, who found me with several magazines, handkerchiefs, pens, and even food in my pockets and under my coat. He reprimanded me thoroughly and lectured me on the dangers of my ways.

"I laid low for two nights, surfaced on the third, and subsequently got caught by a newly installed television alarm in my neighbors' appliance store. This time I was escorted home by two policemen who strongly suggested to my father that I be grounded or locked in the basement for my disorderly conduct. At this point my father shouted, swiftly spanked me, and sent me to my room for an undisclosed amount of time.

"Within a few weeks the dust had settled. I was back on the outside scanning new places for my rip-offs. The spanking didn't alter my desire; it just momentarily curbed it."

Study Questions

1. "I think I would dump your science of behavior in the ocean," Castle says to Frazier. What do you think? Would people gain freedom if the behavioral sciences were discarded? Why? (240)

2. Describe the incident with the falling book of matches. What is Frazier's claim? Castle's claim? Your view? (242)

3. Explain the difference in outcome, according to Frazier, between positive reinforcement and punishment. (244)

4. "Absence of restraint," according to Frazier, "isn't freedom." Explain his viewpoint, including in your answer some reference to his complaint about the vocabulary of freedom. (247)

5. "By a wise choice of techniques," says Frazier, "we *increase* the feeling of freedom." What does he mean? Give an example showing how he might increase a person's feeling of freedom, yet still influence that person's behavior. (248)

6. Castle says: "It's human to dominate in any culture." Frazier replies: "That's an experimental question, Mr. Castle." What does Frazier mean? Explain what he might do. (256)

7. There are four weaknesses in the communist programs in Russia, according to Frazier. What are they? How are they related? (258)

8. Castle is concerned about "general issues" in Walden Two. What does he seem to mean? Explain your answer with references to the different personal styles, thoughts, and interests of Castle and Frazier. (236, 260)

9. What is a fascist? Do you regard Frazier as a fascist? Discuss the use of this word, indicating its advantages and disadvantages. (264)

10. Does Castle feel that any government can function without force? Do you agree? Why? (265)

Values Clarification

The Frazier-Castle dialogues move to Frazier's private room. Time is running short, the question of freedom remains, and Frazier concentrates on the two professors, Castle and Burris.

Freedom does not exist, he declares. The absence of restraint is not freedom. He has some very definite ideas:

1. On who manipulates behavior: "The charlatan, the demagogue, the salesman, the ward healer, the bully, the cheat, the educator, the priest—all who are in possession of the techniques of behavioral engineering." (240)

2. On the need to control behavior: "The fact is, we not only *can* control human behavior, we *must*." (241)

3. On free will: "I deny that freedom exists at all." (241)

4. On positive reinforcement: "By using the principle of positive reinforcement—carefully avoiding force or the threat of force—we can preserve a personal sense of freedom." (248)

These remarks pertain to the philosophical question of free will versus determinism, a most important issue in thinking about a better world. With which comment do you agree most? Write "NOW" preceding that remark.

Think of yourself in ten years or so. With which comment will you agree most at that time? Write "LATER" preceding that comment, which may or may not be the same comment marked earlier.

During adulthood, people change less rapidly than during childhood. Hence, your two responses may be the same. If so, indicate the reasons for your choice and the factors which influenced this constancy. If your choices were different, summarize and explain the reasons for this difference.

Review

The question of free will versus determinism is perhaps the most fundamental issue on which Frazier and Castle disagree, but they have many other differences as well. Reconsider units VI through IX, which focus on their talks, and indicate a basic point of disagreement in each unit.

VI. The Good Life

VII. Politics and Propaganda

VIII. Beyond Heroes

IX. The Question of Freedom

"'We call this ledge the "Throne,"' he said, as he put the glass to his eye. 'Practically all of Walden Two can be seen from it.'"

Unit X
Unfinished Business
(Chapters 32-36)

The basic purpose in this closing unit is to show that behavioral science is unfinished business. Despite his success with Walden Two, Frazier wants to continue, to create a complete science of human behavior, a science as powerful as that of the atom.

Summary

The next morning Castle and Burris pack their bags in preparation for their return to the university. Castle is in a good mood, feeling superior to Frazier, who probably was an academic failure, he decides. Burris realizes that Castle has a marked capacity for self-deception. When the strain of the debate became too great, he simply called Frazier a fascist.

The entire group meets for breakfast, which is uneventful. Afterwards, Frazier invites Burris to join him for his one hour of physical labor. He seems to want to talk privately with Burris, and for lack of an excuse, Burris goes with him to the machine shop, which Frazier is assigned to clean. Frazier enjoys the task, making order out of chaos, despite his untidy personal life.

Burris feels increasingly at ease when he realizes that Frazier is not going to broach the subject of Walden Two. Eventually, he brings it up himself.

He explains that he envies Frazier and perceives him as a genius. Frazier soundly denies his genius, saying that he has no exceptional ability. He was simply persistent, stubborn. He created Walden Two to have things his way.

Burris asks what he will do now that the job is finished, and Frazier becomes angry, pointing out that science is never finished.

"That's nonsense," he replies to Burris. "Can you cite a single instance in the history of science to bear you out? When has a scientific discovery ever made things easy? It may clarify some *former* obscurity or simplify a *former* difficulty, but it always opens up problems which are more obscure and more difficult—and more interesting! Use your imagination, man! Look what remains to be done!"

Frazier is not satisfied with a static culture. He wants to move forward, to build his science of behavior to the point where it can design personalities, control temperament, make a child more mathematical, and improve communal efforts, rather than leaving these outcomes entirely to chance and heredity. The present efficiency of society, he says, is but a fraction of one percent. (Chapter 32)

❧❀❧❀❧❀

With the completion of his hour's work, Frazier leaves the machine shop with a sense of purpose. He leads Burris through a wooded area to a remote spot in the underbrush, at the edge of a cliff. He explains that the spot is called the "Throne," and it overlooks almost all of Walden Two.

For a few minutes Frazier observes the community through a small telescope. Then he lies back and assumes the position of crucifixion, his ankles lightly crossed, arms stretched out, and head resting limply to one side.

This scene upsets Burris, and he expresses the hope that Frazier does not think he is God. Frazier replies: "There's a curious similarity."

The two begin to discuss predestination and free will. Frazier asserts that the behavior of all members of Walden Two is determined, yet they feel free. There is a plan, but they seem to make their own choices and determine the outcomes.

On this basis, Burris accuses Frazier of being a dictator, and Frazier replies that he is less of a dictator than God. In fact, he has improved upon Genesis because he has not had to send a great flood or reveal his plan to people.

Burris resists this comparison, accusing Frazier of a God complex. "Of course I'm not indifferent to power!" replies Frazier. "And I like to play God!"

He takes out his telescope and peers through it for several minutes. "These are my children, Burris." Then he whispers, "I love them."

This statement embarrasses him. "What is love," he shrugs, preparing to leave, "except another name for the use of positive reinforcement?" (Chapter 33)

As Frazier and Burris near the lawn, they hear a disturbance. A sheep has escaped from the portable fold. Even with sheep, Frazier points out, punishment is ineffective in the long term. The string would not be highly successful without the additional presence of the Bishop. Then he compares the control of the dog and the sheep. The former is rewarded, the latter punished, and they behave accordingly. Human society should take note of this difference. Watching the escaped sheep, Castle is amused in a rather forced way. He points out that behavioral engineering is not yet perfect. Frazier glances at Burris, shrugs his shoulders, and walks away. (Chapter 34)

Frazier accepts no expression of thanks as the group prepares to leave, beginning the homeward journey in the community truck. Instead, he reminds everyone of the labor-credits. Mary and Steve, of course, stay at Walden Two.

After a subsequent bus trip, Castle and Burris wait together in the train station, for Barbara and Rodge plan to take another train. Each man is trying to collect his thoughts about Walden Two. Castle maintains a monologue about how someone will stop Frazier before much longer. "It may be the government, it may be rival religious or economic forces, or perhaps just some envious individual inside or outside the community. But someone will get to him, you can be sure of that." He concludes by reciting the demise of several leaders of utopian-type communities. "Look at history, man!"

Lost in his own meditations, Burris is amused by what he thinks would be Frazier's reply. Walden Two has almost nothing in common with those early communities. No comparison can be drawn. They were usually founded on revealed truth; Walden Two is based on scientific principles.

Burris continues his meditations, comparing Frazier and Thoreau. Both agree that there is no purpose in fighting the government. Why try? It is best to let it alone. But Frazier, unlike Thoreau, pays his taxes and compromises when necessary. He has found a route to a better life without trying to alter the world of others.

Castle's words again interrupt Burris' thoughts. "If you really had a technology which could manipulate human behavior," he says, "you could raise some puzzling questions. But isn't that wishful thinking?"

Burris feels otherwise. The techniques of controlling human behavior, he decides, are obvious enough—but possessed by the wrong people. Frazier seems to have evaluated the situation correctly and taken appropriate action. His educational practices, still experimental, are well on the way toward the crucial tests.

Once more, Castle's voice disrupts Burris' private world. "The man's unread," he says, speaking of Frazier. "These things take on a different light when one has read Plato, Rousseau, John Stuart Mill. Frazier needs a good course in the humanities."

Burris, in his own mind, defends Frazier, for nothing arouses him more than the suggestion to abandon science when dealing with human problems. Much of social science, he declares to himself, is unworthy, but it seems preferable to recognize it as nonsense "than to wander around in the all-embracing fog of social philosophy." He is critical of much academic work: "Historical research can take the place of scientific inquiry and give one time out for an honorable snooze, while pretending to carry on."

Castle excuses himself for a moment, and suddenly Burris makes a decision. He checks his bag, dashes out of the train station, and comes to rest on a park bench. He notices a newspaper containing a synopsis of a speech by the president of his university. The president has suggested worthwhile educational goals, but Burris realizes that he has no idea how to achieve them. At almost the same time, he suddenly realizes that he will go back to Walden Two.

Burris travels unencumbered returning to Walden Two, with a few essentials in his knapsack, taken from his bag, and a newly purchased copy of *Walden* in his pocket. He begins his walk disappointed that it is not raining or night, which would better fit his heroic mood. Instead, he walks along the sidewalks on a warm day. (Chapter 35)

Finally arriving at Walden Two, Burris is met by Steve Jamnik, who is not surprised to see him. "Mr. Frazier told me you were coming back," he says.

The astonished Burris glances fearfully up at the Throne. He is gratified to find that Frazier is not there. (Chapter 36)

Key Concepts

Write a definition for each of these terms. When in doubt, reread the indicated pages in *Walden Two* and consult the glossary in this guidebook.

static culture, 273

science of human behavior, 274

communal science, 275

noncompetitive intelligence, 280

threat of pain, 283

Thoreauvian, 289

Illustrations

The concepts in *Walden Two* are often illustrated in daily life. Below are students' illustrations of three concepts in this unit. Supply additional examples yourself of these or other key concepts in this unit.

Noncompetitive intelligence (280). "In my high school, which was a private school, individual competition was avoided, insofar as possible.

"In the classroom, there were no grades in the traditional sense and whenever our work was evaluated, it was a mutual effort between teacher and student, and then the teacher wrote a paragraph or page which summarized the discussion. If the student felt differently about the outcome, he or she wrote another statement which was included with the report.

"Out on the playing fields, all the activities were non-zero sum games, meaning that the scores made by one person or one team were not counted as points against the other side. Both 'teams' could score points at the same time. The 'for' and 'against' scores did not add up to zero. Usually we played 'catch' or ran as a group or tried to keep a large ball bouncing into the air as long as possible. Sometimes, we all ran in the rain, trying not to get wet. In winter, we slid or made designs in the snow. Naturally, the frisbee was always a popular item.

"After I left, the school closed. I guess parents did not want to send their kids, probably because they really did not know what it was all about. Many of my friends from that school are actively involved in disarmament and are trying to encourage a noncompetitive approach to the work environment. They have jobs of this sort, and of course they serve as models for their own children. The basic principle of non-competition seems to be a permanent part of their lives.

"Those of us in college do not seem to have any problems—or any more than students from competitive schools—probably because competition is such a fundamental part of American life.

"In any case, I think that my school has improved the world in a small way. What we need are more such schools—not less—for world survival depends on the way people are trained to look at life, especially at other people, as companions or rivals."

Threat of pain (283). "In high school I hated living with my parents. I was 'permanently grounded' after dinner, except on Friday and Saturday nights. I couldn't go out unless I showed them, in full detail, that I had done *all* my homework. After solitary confinement with the books, and a successful plea, I was paroled until ten o'clock. It really made me mad. My parents were wardens, the house a prison. I wasn't physically restrained, but the threat of force and pain was constantly there.

"My friend Aniko worked no less on her homework but felt very different about it. She lived with her uncle, a laid-back man who trusted himself and Aniko as well. He simply told her to go out and enjoy herself as soon as she finished her studies. During that year our evenings out and efforts at homework were about the same. In fact, we often went out together.

"But we had very different feelings about what had happened. Homework for me was a means of escaping a bad situation. My parents' approach simply made me do the work. It didn't develop in me any interest in studying. Now in college, where they're not around, I don't do any studying at all."

Thoreauvian (289). "Martin lives in another world. No bank account, no car, no driver's license, no credit cards—of course. He carries what money he earns in his pocket and always seems to have enough for his tastes—bread, wine, and fish.

"He's a free-lance carpenter, usually working independently on some private job in the country. He has no interest in business, advancement, or especially becoming somebody's boss or worker. Naturally, he has no interest in government or politics.

"'Voting is a waste of time,' he says. 'Your vote doesn't mean a thing.' But he says he would in a small election—if a suitable candidate came along. So far, no one has met his approval—so he's not even registered to exercise his option!"

Study Questions

1. "And you've had the fun of being a pioneer," says Burris of Frazier's success in establishing Walden Two. "You've skimmed the cream. It's going to be all too easy for those who follow." How does Frazier respond? Cite an example from the history of science to support his view. (272)

2. Frazier cannot be satisfied with a static culture. "Science must go on," he says. What does he mean? In what specific areas is further development most necessary? (273)

3. Frazier wants to make people happy, to develop a productive society, and to make possible a true science of human behavior. Which of these is most important to him? Why? (274)

4. What does Frazier mean by communal science? To what extent does it exist already? How might it be developed further? (275)

5. Behavior is determined, claims Frazier, yet people can still feel free. How is this possible? (279)

6. Love, according to Frazier, is simply another word for what principle? Do you agree? Why or why not? (282)

7. "It's a primitive principle of control," Frazier says of punishment. Why does he take this position? (283)

8. Why does Frazier feel the sheep will need frequent punishment or an unsurmountable fence in order to be contained? Why does the Bishop control the sheep without punishment? Focus upon the different goals of the sheep, the dog, and also humanity. (283)

9. In the bus station, Burris suddenly changes his course of action, deciding to return to Walden Two. Is this decision a demonstration of free will or determinism? Explain your answer. (292)

10. When Burris returns to Walden Two, he glances towards the Throne, relieved to find no one there. Why? What do you suppose Frazier is doing at that moment? (301)

Values Clarification

With no chance of converting Castle, Frazier lures Burris to his workshop and then to the Throne. He turns to the most important topics in their previous discussions:

1. On world survival: "The discrepancy between man's technical power and the wisdom with which he uses it has grown conspicuously wider year by year." (273)

2. On questions of happiness: "We can study them only in a living culture, and yet a culture which is under experimental control." (274)

3. On the capacity of behavioral technology: "Give me the specifications and I'll give you the man." (274)

4. On punishment: "It's a primitive principle of control." (283)

Apart from Frazier's remarks, which topic is most important to you? Mark it with your name. After thinking about Frazier's comments, identify the topic which seems most important to him. Mark it with his name. Finally, write Castle's name before the topic he would consider most critical. These choices need not be mutually exclusive. Any or all names may be placed beside any topic.

Discuss the similarities and differences among these choices, referring to the personalities, if appropriate. Include the reasons for your own position and note any conditions which might prompt you to change your reaction.

Review

Consider the entire contents of *Walden Two* and then match the statements in the right-hand column with the titles in the left-hand column. Fill in each blank with the proper Roman numeral.

I. Breaking Away

II. Design of Things

III. Working, Playing

IV. Raising Children

V. Marriage and the Family

VI. The Good Life

VII. Politics and Propaganda

VIII. Beyond Heroes

IX. The Question of Freedom

X. Unfinished Business

_____ The leader or personal figure supplements a faulty science of human behavior.

_____ Children have increased feelings of security in the group-care context.

_____ Scientific discovery always opens up new problems which are more interesting and more difficult.

_____ New lambs never question the judgment of their elders.

_____ It entails health, minimal unpleasant labor, opportunity to exercise talents, satisfactory personal contacts, and relaxation.

_____ The physical environment influences behavior; improvements are sought in all spheres of life.

_____ Behavior can be controlled by situations that create positive outcomes.

_____ Credits serve as currency; people can earn enough in half a day

_____ The proper approach involves experimentation, not indoctrination.

_____ Lessons should be administered in carefully graded sequences, not accidental doses.

Appendix Notes.

 1

 2

 3

Appendix
Persons, Places, and Events

Persons (in order of appearance)

Lieutenant "Rodge" Rogers	Recently discharged from military service (1)
Professor Burris	Rogers' former psychology instructor (1)
Lieutenant Steve Jamnik	Also recently discharged, a friend of Rogers (1)
Professor Augustine Castle	Instructor in philosophy, Burris' colleague (8)
Barbara Macklin	Fiancée of Rogers (9)
Mary Grove	Girlfriend of Jamnik (10)
T. E. Frazier	Tour guide, "founder" of Walden Two (11)
Mrs. Rachel Meyerson	Manager of clothing for women (24)
Woman at the Work Desk	Responsible for work assignments (64)
Dairy Manager	In charge of cows, milk, fodder, manure (70)
Mrs. Nash	Guide for the Lower and Upper Nurseries (86)
Mr. Meyerson	Physician in the medical building (175)
Miss Ely	Dentist in the dental office (176)
Mrs. Olson	Pastry cook (204)
Telegraphic clerk	In the railroad station (295)

Places

Main buildings	Interconnected quarters for sleeping, dining, and recreation (13)
Visitors' rooms	Containing one or two bunks, a hinged table, small clothes closet, recessed shelves and cupboards, and one or two comfortable chairs (13)
Front lawn	An expanse of grass with sheep (15)
Pond	Former swamp containing clear, fresh water (17)
Truck gardens	Beyond the pond and its dam (17)
Pine grove	To screen the workshops from the main buildings (17)
Strip of birches	Supplying firewood and separating the gardens from the regular sheep pasture (17)
The Ladder	A long passageway with many windows, connecting the children's quarters and main buildings (20)
Alcove	A stopping place in the Ladder for having tea, chatting, or resting (24)
The Walk	A broad, curving corridor running the full length of the main building (34)
Dining rooms	Small and decorated in different styles: efficiency, early American, English, colorful Swedish decor (40)
Utility room for dishwashing	Accommodating just two workers (42)
Lounges	For reading, music, and conversation, furnished with chairs, rugs, and heavy pillows for use on the floor (45)
Common rooms	Used for administrative functions, such as the Work Desk (64)
The dairy	The most modern section of the farm (70)
Stone Hill	A steep hill with natural caves some distance from the main buildings, formerly a stone quarry (70)
Deodorizing building	A small dressing area for dealing with objectionable farm odors, illustrating social engineering (71)
Bulletin board	Describing in small print all the meetings, parties, concerts, matches and other entertainment available to community members and guests (77)
Theatre	Containing a stage and makeshift podium but no orchestra pit (84)
Lower nursery	A series of small rooms lined with air-conditioned cubicles, each cubicle containing a baby visible through a large window (87)
Upper nursery	For children aged one to three years, with playrooms, lavatory, a dressing room, several sleeping rooms, and recreation areas outdoors (91)

The noninstitutional "school building"	Workshops, laboratories, studies, and reading rooms used in an open, informal manner for the education of the children (108)
Flower gardens	Near the main buildings, adjacent to the lawn (119)
Personal room	A separate room for one person—a husband, wife or any other adult—especially after the period of childbearing (128, 146)
Roof of the common rooms	With deck and beach chairs for enjoying the daytime and evening weather (146)
Medical building	On a plateau above the Ladder, emphasizing preventive medicine and dentistry (175)
Frazier's personal room	A room in great confusion, showing the occupant's disorderly personal habits (231)
Locker room	Containing all the heavy outdoor clothing, for rain and cold, including a "dirt trap" at the entrance (261)
The Throne	A ledge on the upper rim of Stone Hill giving a panoramic view of the whole community (277)

Events

Wednesday morning	The touring party—Professors Burris and Castle and the two young couples—depart for Walden Two. (11)
Three o'clock Wednesday	After resting from their trip, the group is invited by Frazier for a leisurely walk to the pond, during which he points out the natural features of Walden Two and the environmental improvements the community has made, including the lawn maintained by sheep and the reclamation of the pond. (14)
Tea time, Wednesday	Near the top of the Ladder, the visitors enjoy refreshments from pail-like tea glasses and square dishes, examples of domestic engineering in Walden Two. (25)
Wednesday, seven o'clock	Frazier meets the group for dinner, showing the Walk and lounge rooms enroute, describing the staggered schedule for meals, work, and entertainment, an instance of cultural engineering. (34)
Wednesday evening	The group finds a small lounge off the Walk where Frazier describes the work force and labor credits in Walden Two. (45)
Thursday morning	After breakfast, the visitors report to the Work Desk, receive an assignment, and earn their first labor credits by washing windows. (60)
After lunch, Thursday	A truck ride provides an easy visit to the farm area and workshops, and Frazier points with pride to the deodorizing buildings, a special achievement in social engineering. (68)
Thursday evening	Following a discussion of the arts at dinner, the group attends a brief concert presented by the community members. (79)
Friday morning	Visits to the Lower and Upper Nurseries and the noninstitutional "school" building occupy the guests, who hear Frazier describe methods for developing in children a tolerance for frustration, self-control, and resistance to discouragement. (86)
Noon, Friday	Having lunch at a small table in the English inn, the group discusses sex problems and early marriage, topics prompted by an encounter with a teen-age couple and their baby. (121)
After lunch, Friday	Sitting or leaning on leather cushions on the floor of one of the lounges, the visitors listen to Frazier discuss community love in Walden Two, which practices free affection and a communal approach to child rearing. (128)
Mid-afternoon, Friday	The visitors earn labor credits by stacking wood and lighter work. (138)
Friday, seven o'clock	Burris arrives late to dinner, after which the group moves to deck and beach chairs on the roof of the common rooms, where Frazier presents his view of the good life, the Walden Code, and the experimental point of view. (142)

Saturday, breakfast	Barbara explains that Steve and Mary are joining Walden Two, an announcement which draws mixed reactions. (172)
Noon, Saturday	After two hours washing windows, the group proceeds to the medical buildings, where Steve and Mary take the medical admissions tests, everyone tours the facilities, and Frazier speaks of preventive medicine and dentistry. (175)
Lunch, Saturday	Frazier announces that the tour of the community is completed and a lengthy discussion on human nature ensues, focusing upon issues in government, religion, and public relations. (179)
Saturday, after lunch	On shaded benches outside the dining rooms, the visitors listen to Frazier's views on indoctrination and propaganda, as opposed to experimentation. (191)
Four o'clock Saturday	Burris decides to sample the behavior of the community members, progressing from stage to stage on the Ladder, invariably with positive findings and then, enroute to his room, encounters Mrs. Olson in the gardens, again with favorable results. (197)
Saturday evening	The arrival of an advance guard from Walden Six prompts a discussion in one of the common rooms about government, history, fascism, personal figures, and the dissemination of Walden Two's ideas. (208)
Sunday morning	While all the others are at a Sunday church service, Burris and Frazier go to the latter's untidy private room, where he confesses personal shortcomings and complains that he is not a product of Walden Two. (227)
Sunday afternoon	With the young couples at a concert, Burris and Frazier go again to the latter's room, this time with Castle, and here they discuss Castle's general issues, including the question of freedom, with Frazier emphasizing determinism. (236)
After supper, Sunday	Frazier goes off with Rodge, whom he fails to convert, leaving Castle to grade students' papers and Burris to think long thoughts of Walden Two and "time's winged chariot." (264)
Monday morning	Burris reluctantly accompanies Frazier to his work at the machine shop, and then to the Throne, where Frazier surveys the entire community, speaks of its members as his children, and speaks of love as positive reinforcement. (267)
Noon Monday	One of the sheep escapes from the portable fold, prompting Castle to gloat, Frazier to become annoyed, and a small commotion in the community. (283)
After lunch, Monday	The touring party bids goodbye and boards a community truck for the trip to the bus station and thence to the train. (286)
Thursday noon	Burris arrives again at Walden Two, having walked sixty miles from the railroad station, and he looks up at the Throne, relieved to find that Frazier is not there. (301)

Glossary of Key Concepts

The Roman numeral after each term indicates the unit in this guidebook. The Arabic number indicates a page in *Walden Two*.

behavioral engineering I, 10   Broadly, any method for controlling behavior. Specifically, the use of reinforcement principles to modify the behavior of an individual. For example, through behavioral engineering an individual may learn to stop smoking. Compare with cultural engineering.

communal science X, 275   A group effort at scientific inquiry. Twentieth-century science is generally regarded as a communal enterprise. In Walden Two, the aim is to develop communal art, music, and literature, as well, under the assumption that the effort of the group may be more productive than the separate efforts of the individuals.

community love IV, 90   Love of everyone, especially of children. Caring for children by all members of a community. Compare with free affection.

competitive society VIII, 216   A social group with rivalry among its members for resources and opportunities. Individual gains are made at others' expense. Compare with cooperative society.

conditioned reflex III, 77   A prompt, involuntary response, aroused by some stimulus which does not naturally evoke it. An individual becomes excited when reading the bulletin board, after it has been paired previously with interesting, pleasant entertainment.

conspicuous consumption II, 30   The use of goods and resources chiefly to demonstrate wealth. Unnecessary acquisitions and expenditures.

control of weather I, 19   The idea that behavior is controlled in part by the weather. Adverse weather prompts people to wear special clothes, stay indoors, change plans, and become ill. Favorable weather is less coercive. In Walden Two, the personal rooms, dining rooms, common rooms, libraries, and theaters are all connected, allowing events to take place without regard for the weather.

controls VI, 163   Holding certain factors constant in order to study the influence of other factors. The influence of A on B is determined by eliminating, or holding constant, all other factors.

cooperative housing I, 19   Living facilities designed for sharing, especially by large groups. The aim is economic savings and the simplification of living conditions.

cooperative society IX, 245   A social group based upon mutual advantage; no member makes a gain at the expense of another member. Sharing work and responsibility for the benefit of all. Compare with competitive society.

cultural engineering II, 38   Methods for controlling the behavior of a large group of people, chiefly through the use of reinforcement principles. Some behaviors controlled in this way include work level, motivation, emotional reactions, and self-control. For example, through cultural engineering there may be no smoking at all in a given society. Compare with behavioral engineering. See reinforcement theory.

democracy VIII, 217   Government based on majority rule. The choice of its members is expressed directly or through representatives.

design a series of adversities IV, 105   To prepare a program of successive experiences for children, each slightly more difficult, or adverse, than its predecessor. A graded process; after each adversity is successfully met, the next-most-difficult is encountered. Walden Two children learn frustration tolerance in this gradual fashion, step by step, each delay slightly longer or more difficult than the preceding one. See tolerance for frustration.

despotism IX, 238   Absolute authority; the exercise of total power over others; a form of tyranny.

domestic engineering II, 25   Arranging the environment to make household tasks easier and to increase enjoyment of life around the home. The tea service in Walden Two is constructed to avoid spillings, save effort in refilling, and have an aesthetic appearance. Compare with industrializing housewifery.

environment IV, 107   One's surroundings; the total circumstances in which an individual exists, including physical, social, emotional, intellectual, and other factors.

experiment I, 5   A test or examination, an investigation; to try something new, to manipulate variables in order to study their influences.

experimental attitude II, 25   A preference for testing an idea, rather than speculating; a predisposition for obtaining direct evidence in support or refutation of some viewpoint. Near synonym for experimental point of view.

experimental point of view VI, 162   The view that problems can be solved by doing experiments, by making direct tests of an hypothesis or idea. Near synonym for experimental attitude.

experimental question IV, 103   A question which can or should be answered by a direct test; a problem requiring an empirical solution, obtained through experience. See experiment.

family V, 128   The fundamental social group; persons related by blood or marriage. A nuclear family consists of parents and children; the extended family includes other relatives. In Walden Two, the entire community replaces the nuclear and even the extended family.

fascism VIII, 219   A dictatorship, involving extreme conservatism and chauvinistic views.

free affection V, 129   Unrestricted expression of tender feelings toward other adults of either sex; displays of fondness for people without regard for social convention. Compare with community love.

freedom IX, 240   Absence of restraints; complete independence from all force or control. In Walden Two, freedom is regarded as an illusion, a feeling which arises when the control involves positive reinforcement. See positive reinforcement.

the Good Life VI, 146   Ideal or optimal conditions for human living, defined in Walden Two as good health, a minimum of unpleasant labor, opportunities to use talents and abilities, satisfying personal relationships, and adequate rest and relaxation.

human engineering VII, 181   A general term referring to procedures for controlling human behavior. See behavioral engineering, cultural engineering.

human nature VII, 182   Intrinsic personal characteristics. Since it is difficult or impossible to measure inborn human characteristics, completely unaffected by experience, this term usually refers to personal qualities as modified by the environment. In Walden Two, little faith is placed in human nature, apart from environmental influences. For example, it is not assumed that people are innately good or evil; rather, they are shaped by experience.

identification V, 134 The process of adopting the attitudes, interests, and behaviors of another person, usually an older person.

indoctrination VII, 191 Instruction in a certain viewpoint, usually without critical thought; teaching which does not include a balanced perspective. In Walden Two, the aim is to arrive at a certain viewpoint through experimentation, not indoctrination.

industrializing housewifery II, 43 Organizing of household tasks for greater mechanization, efficiency, and mass production. Eight or ten people, working in pairs for one shift each, do the dishwashing for all one thousand members of Walden Two. Compare with domestic engineering.

labor credits III, 45 A form of money; entries in a ledger indicating hours of work. Each member of Walden Two contributes four credits per day in exchange for the goods and services of the community. The value of the credit, currently one hour, changes with the needs of the community.

the "Ladder" I, 20 A hillside passageway with many windows, stairs, benches, and furnished alcoves connecting the children's quarters and main lounging rooms.

longitudinal study VII, 203 Observing closely one or more individuals for an extended period. A longitudinal study typically extends over several years, not over a day or so.

Managers III, 48 Specialists who have administrative functions, serving as Managers of Food, Health, Play, Arts, Labor, Education, and other divisions of the community. They supervise the Scientists, responsible for applied research, and all Workers, who constitute the rest of the labor force in Walden Two, except for the Planners. The Workers repair teeth, dig ditches, care for children, design buildings, pick corn, fix engines, and do all kinds of other jobs. See also Planners.

noncompetitive intelligence X, 280 Mental ability used for the common good, devoted to the benefit of all rather than to individual gain. See competitive society, cooperative society.

objective sampling VII, 197 An unbiased procedure for obtaining information from a few people, presumably representative of a larger group.

personal figures VIII, 221 Any great person in history; a leader or hero. According to Walden Two, a personal figure arises when the government, or behavioral science, is inadequate. The government of Walden Two contains several guarantees against the emergence of any community leader.

Philistinism III, 78 Conventionalism; ignorance; smugness; a lack of interest in artistic and cultural values.

Planners III, 48 The government of Walden Two, involving three men and three women. They make policies, have certain judicial responsibilities, and review the work of the Managers, who promote them for office. See Managers.

positive reinforcement IX, 244 Presenting a positive stimulus, such as food or fresh air, thereby increasing the probability of a given response.

prescientific days V, 131   Before the rise of modern science, usually before the seventeenth-century work of Sir Francis Bacon. Behavioral science is generally considered a twentieth-century development.

preventive dentistry VI, 177   Procedures for avoiding dental problems. Fluoridation of drinking water for children is an example. See preventive medicine.

preventive medicine VI, 176   Health practices aimed at avoiding illnesses before they occur. In contrast, curative medicine deals with problems which have already arisen. See preventive dentistry.

propaganda VII, 194   Information promoting a certain viewpoint, disseminated in behalf of a specific doctrine.

punishment IX, 244   Presenting a negative stimulus, such as spanking the child. Immediately, this treatment may delay or prevent the undesired response because some incompatible behavior has been evoked. The child stops tormenting the cat because he is crying instead. In the long term, it may prompt avoidance reactions in the child, including undesirable side effects, and if the punishment ceases, the behavior may reappear.

reinforcement theory IX, 244   The view that behavior is influenced by its consequences; behaviors followed by favorable consequences tend to be repeated and those followed by neutral or unfavorable consequences tend to be discarded. See positive reinforcement, punishment.

representative sample II, 28   A portion of a group or whole which accurately depicts the larger body. A representative sample can be obtained in several ways. When all the items or parts have an equal chance of being included in a large sample, usually that sample is representative.

science of human behavior X, 274   Application of the scientific method—forming, testing, and verifying hypotheses—to the study of human activity. Generally, the late nineteenth century is considered to mark the beginning of the modern, empirical approach to the study of human behavior.

"self-control" IV, 96   Management of one's own feelings and actions, presumably through will power. In Walden Two it is assumed that this power or control comes originally from the environment. See design of adversities, tolerance for frustration.

sex problem V, 121   Any difficulty in connection with reproductive functions. In Walden Two, teen-aged individuals are assumed to be ready for the natural expression of sexual impulses; they are permitted to marry and have children, thereby avoiding many sex problems which arise through unnatural social restrictions on these activities.

social conscience V, 140   A concern for the welfare of others, especially with regard to food, clothing, shelter, and living conditions.

social engineering III, 71   Use of reinforcement principles for controlling the behavior of a large group of people. Synonym for cultural engineering.

static culture X, 273   An unchanging society; a culture without progress or evolution. In Walden Two it is assumed that successful cultures are not static; they develop through experimentation.

Thoreauvian X, 289   In the manner of Henry David Thoreau, who resisted perceived wrongs in government by refusing to pay taxes, living alone in the woods.

threat of pain   X, 283   An aversive stimulus used to coerce behavior; a menacing situation; potential punishment.

tolerance for frustration   IV, 88   Capacity to accept delay or thwarting of gratification; accepting certain goals as unattainable, temporarily or permanently. See design of adversities.

utopian community   I, 2   An ideal society; a place approaching perfection, named for the imaginary setting described in Thomas More's sixteenth-century work.

Walden   VIII, 209   A pond in Massachusetts and the title of a book by Henry David Thoreau describing his experiment in living alone in nature near the pond.

the Walden Code   VI, 150   Rules of conduct in Walden Two. A trivial rule: Do not discuss affairs of the community with outsiders. A more important rule: Explain your work to any interested community member.

Walden Six   VIII, 208   A community founded by members of Walden Two, based on the principles of Walden Two. Seemingly related communities, Waldens Three, Four, and Five, tried to follow the Walden Two model but were not settled by experienced members of Walden Two.

Bibliography

All works cited in *Walden Two*, except those on morals and ethics, appear here. Also included are related writings by B. F. Skinner.

Bacon, Francis. *New Atlantis*. Arlington Heights, Illinois: Harlan Davidson, 1980.

First published in London in 1627, Bacon's utopia is set on an island in the South Sea. Fifty-one lost sailors encounter a mode of life beyond the Old and New Worlds. Solomon's House is the most important institution; it houses a learned society which applies the scientific method to problems of daily life. A happy civilization is the result, demonstrating Bacon's faith in the potentiality of science for improving the human condition. (9, 179)

Bellamy, Edward. *Looking Backward*. New York: New American Library, 1982.

The city of Boston in 2000 is the setting for this utopian fiction, published in 1888. Bellamy believed that human beings are fundamentally good; our evil ways arise through inept and discriminatory social practices. In this ideal society, the Industrial Army is a most important institution, a way of organizing human activity, especially in the economic sphere, for greater justice and the greater benefit of all. (9, 19, 46, 179)

Butler, Samuel. *Erewhon*. New York: Penguin, 1970.

This title comes from "nowhere" spelled almost backwards. The place is England, and the presentation satirical, aimed at the hypocrisy, stupidity and malpractices in 1872. The Religion of the Musical Banks ridicules churches and business; the College of Unreason belittles academics; the Rights of Vegetables shows the author's interest in plant research. Butler's wit is prominent and still relevant. (159, 179)

Hilton, James. *Lost Horizon*. New York: Pocket Books, 1984.

A new word, Shangri-La, meaning a place of eternal happiness, entered our language in 1933 when Hilton described this imaginary land beyond the Himalayas. Four passengers, kidnapped in a special airplane, find the secret of long life and contentment in Shangri-La, but no visitor can leave. The hero, forced by his three companions to escape, suffers from exhaustion and hallucinations and tries to return to Shangri-La. (9, 179)

More, Thomas. *Utopia*. New York: Norton, 1975.

Appearing originally in Latin in 1516, More's work was the first significant utopian literature since Plato and gave its name to the concept. It describes the injustices and inequalities in contemporary England, in sharp contrast with Utopia, where the key to the good life is moderation. All citizens except the most erudite work a six-hour day, without hostility or excess, guided by a benevolent, unpretentious king. This description became an important commentary on the social and economic problems in the industrialization of England. (9)

Morris, William. *News from Nowhere*. New York: Penguin, 1984.

Inspired by Bellamy's work, Morris moves to the Middle Ages, rather than the year 2000. The simple folk of this socialist community live a peaceful, rather leisurely existence, gratified by successful artisanship and brotherly love. This outcome does not arise through careful social organization, with sophisticated political and economic planning, but rather through humanity's natural inclination towards love and beauty, which becomes manifest when it goes unfettered. (147, 165, 179)

Plato. *The Republic*. Buffalo, New York: Prometheus Books, 1986.

In Athens in the fourth century B.C., Plato describes his ideal, the loftiest culture in classical philosophy. As the author says, it belongs more in heaven than on earth, but it contains the basic themes of most subsequent utopian literature. The chief figure is Socrates, the narrator, whose critical thought demonstrates the Socratic method at its best. His dialogues with friends, before silent listeners, address such difficult questions as the ideal state and the nature of justice. (9)

Skinner, B. F. *About Behaviorism*. New York: Knopf, 1974.

Written largely in lay language, the author clarifies his position. Twenty misstatements about behaviorism appear at the beginning, and they are reconsidered at the conclusion. Particularly concerned about global issues, Skinner asserts that humanity controls its own destiny. Thus, he presents the philosophy of his science of behavior, offered as a promising approach in the solution of the major problems in today's world.

Skinner, B. F. *The Behavior of Organisms: An Experimental Analysis*. New York: Appleton-Century-Crofts, 1966.

This volume, with a preface to the seventh edition, is a reprint of the author's first book. It presents his early laboratory research and contains a major new emphasis at the time, a shift from respondent to operant behavior, evident in most of Skinner's later work. In the year of publication, 1938, he refused to extrapolate beyond the laboratory. Seven years later, he published *Walden Two* speculating on the application of his principles.

Skinner, B. F. "News from Nowhere, 1984." *The Behavior Analyst*, 8, 5-14, 1985.

A man claiming to be Eric Arthur Blair, better known as George Orwell, author of *Nineteen Eighty-Four*, joined Walden Two in 1950. He had some lengthy discussions with Frazier on government, religion, depersonalization, the "hippie movements," labor-saving devices, gambling, the welfare system, advantages of small communities, conservation of the environment, and world survival. These dialogues, reported by Burris, provide Skinner with an opportunity for updating and expanding on the ideas in *Walden Two*.

Veblen, Thorstein. *Theory of the Leisure Class*. Boston: Houghton Mifflin, 1973.

From the pen of a liberal, humorous economist in 1899, this book is not utopian fiction. It is a statement about the leisure class in modern society. Persons with even a small extra income, beyond survival, the author argues, use these funds to impress other people, not to better their own or others' lives. "Conspicuous consumption" is the best known concept emerging from this work, for which the theoretical basis was laid in a series of articles in an early volume of the *American Journal of Sociology*. (15)

Wells, H. G. *A Modern Utopia*. Lincoln: University of Nebraska Press, 1967.

No kidnapping or shipwreck brings on this utopian experience but rather a person sitting at his desk reading. His own imagination takes him to a path high in the Alps where he meets a botanist consumed with thoughts of a lady he loves and the plight of dogs. Their discussions of a utopian community are constantly interrupted by the scientist's excursions into his earthly problems, but Wells' 1905 message is clear. Utopia must be a world society; anything less than a world-wide community, with complete centralization, will be inadequate. (19)

Index for *Walden Two*

All concepts, terms, authors, and their works cited in *Walden Two* appear in this index. These page numbers refer to *Walden Two*, not to this guidebook.